Ling & Lamb ──────

Beautiful
FOOLISHNESS

Copyright © Ling & Lamb Publishing, 2025. All rights reserved.

Dedication

*This book is dedicated to our Ling and Lamb Fam.
And to those who don't know us...*

Welcome to the Famington.

What Fans Are Saying About Ling and Lamb

Comments and messages from real viewers and fans!

> Good morning I love watching your love story over and over, I am 75 years old, been married, now a widow, miss my love. u bring so much life back to me Thank you keep on loving each other forever 🩶

> Hey Ling & Lamb you both are such beautiful people and yes she is a beautiful queen, I just want you both to know much you inspire me everyday to live, love and laugh. You all are a ray of sunshine 😊 and joy in my life and I want you to keep bringing joy to people who would not otherwise know joy. We love and support what you do to the fullest.

> I'm watching from Cape Town South Africa 🇿🇦 Love love you guys! Keep them coming 🇿🇦

> I would just like to let you know that I love the two of you. I see the love that you have for each other, in every video that you do. Some of the videos have made me laugh so much that I was in tears. Thank you for sharing your good times with the world. God bless and keep you both safe xx

> I absolutely LOVE you two!! Whenever I see you two, my heart is filled with joy and laughter!!

> I have never ever ever laughed so hard in all my life 😂😂😂😂😂 you both are amazing xxx so much love from the uk 🩶🩶🩶

> I was having a bad day. Thank God for you guys you made me laugh. Nceone.

> Hey Ling and Lamb you both are such beautiful people and yes she is a beautiful queen, I just want you both to know how much you inspire me everyday to live, love and laugh. You all are a ray of sunshine and joy in my life and I want you to keep bringing joy to people who would not otherwise know joy. We love and support what you do to the fullest.

> I love ur relationship. I don't think u realize how much u have opened up people to cultural foods!! And creating an amazing relationship and connecting through food it's so amazing!!

> Hello guys ... Marcus from Singapore ... Really love you guys!!!

> lool you guys are too funny ... new subscriber and Ling & Lamb Fan .. all the way from Jamaica. love your chemistry

> I'm a subscriber off Youtube and I love your channel just wanted to send a big hug to you both. Praying always for you and wishing you both a peaceful day today

> Love you guys and your vibe is amazing! By the way Lamb I 😊 your newest song actually all of your music

> I love y'all's videos! Stay blessed

> Thank you so much. Much love!! 🤍

Table of Contents

A Culture Shock Welcome Party	9
Chapter One: A Childhood of Memories/An Introduction to Ling and Lamb	17
Chapter Two: The Power of Self-Care/Loving Yourselves Enhances Your Love For Each Other	39
Chapter Three: Fulfilling Our Destiny/Embracing the Journey	55
Chapter Four: It's a Lifetime Journey, Not A One Night Stand/Learning And Unlearning	71
Chapter Five: Keeping It REAL/Communication With Your Partner	87
Chapter Six: Teamwork Makes The Dream Work/Together We Thrive, Achieving More as One	103
Chapter Seven: The Application of Patience/Master The Art Of Waiting	117
Chapter Eight: When The Pancake Hits You Back/Turning Setbacks into Stepping Stones for Success	133
Chapter Nine: You Had The Power All Along/Intentional Living	149
Chapter Ten: What You Say Is What You Get/The Power of Words	169
Chapter Eleven: Not All That Glitters Is Gold Happiness in a Social Media World	181
Conclusion	197
Acknowledgments	204
About the Authors	209

Introduction

A Culture Shock Welcome Party

"When you give joy to other people, you get more joy in return. You should give a good thought to happiness that you can give out."

— *Eleanor Roosevelt, first lady of the United States from 1933 to 1945*

Lamb

When I first came to the United States, it was for a fundraising concert that had been organized by a show promoter and a church. The funds raised during that show would be used for my prison reform movement back in Nigeria. The cultural shock I experienced during that first visit was my welcome party.

Everything from mannerisms, behaviors, the tone of my voice, to even food. There were so many differences that it was hard for me to adjust right away. I realized that culture, even my culture, is not superior to others.

I come from a place where what the man says is final. When a woman from a different culture enters into a marriage, she is expected to adopt the culture of her husband. The woman's culture dies. Even when the couple has kids, they are taught their father's culture. This is what I had been taught from a young age and saw happen in my own family.

Yet, there I was in the United States. Thousands of miles away from my home. During that fundraising concert, I met Ling's mother who was working with the event organizer. She was tagging everyone on Facebook to help promote that event. Including me. It was through that interaction that I stumbled upon a photo of Ling on Facebook and immediately knew that one day she would be my wife. Not just my girlfriend. My wife. One of the funniest parts of this story is that I hadn't realized that who I was interacting with was Ling's mom at the time. I had just seen a photo of Ling and knew that it was fate shooting an arrow at my heart

To be honest, my friends thought I had gone mad. They wanted to know how I knew that a beautiful woman I had never met before would one day become my wife. I knew it deep within my soul and proceeded with that confidence.

During that trip, I had also planned to shoot a music video. I spoke with Ling's mom, asking her if she could get me in touch with Ling. She said I would have to ask her myself, and that's how I finally was able to meet Ling in person. When I reached out to Ling on Instagram DM, I could tell she was hesitant at first, but she finally agreed and we connected, the rest became history. That music video is still on YouTube today.

I married Ling, a beautiful, American woman that is from a totally opposite cultural belief. When people see us together, both in-person and on social media, they often ask us how we can be so much in love and experience satisfaction when we come from completely different worlds. Even after what people call the 'honeymoon' phase has passed for us, we still treat each other with as much love, and perhaps even more, as when we were first married. It is our love for each other and that silliness we express that has become the foundation of everything we do. And what we would like to share with the world.

Scan to see music video.

Ling

The one thing we've learned from our viewers by reading their comments and direct messages is that everyone appreciates how we treat one another. Even amongst all the silly pranks I play on Lamb, it is good to see how we are able to spark so much joy and laughter in the lives of others. We receive so many questions asking us how we can truly be in this much love for one another. I believe many of our viewers wonder if what we have is actually real.

What we discovered before we were ever married is that fulfillment is experienced once you discover things in life that you are truly passionate about. Not necessarily what will make you the most money. When you live a life following the things you love, it will lead you to the prosperity you are yearning for. Lamb and I both follow our passions, and it has led to the life we have consciously created together.

When we married, our joy for life only grew. In fact, we often describe it as explosive ' as we learned to communicate with one another, respect each other's cultural differences, and support one another with our own individual passions and goals.

Social media has been a great outlet for us to showcase the happiness we experience, the passionate love we have for one another, and also how we can still be silly even though we've been married for years. However, social media isn't always the best example of love and well-being because the big stories highlighted are often covering the negative side to relationships. There are even some who are afraid to enter into a relationship because social media is filled with "break up" stories and "hold your nose, love is in the air" sentiments.

Lamb

We'll be honest with you. This book might reveal why you are missing fulfillment in your relationship, and what true love really is. We are firm believers that any couple can experience the deep love, joy, and passion we experience every day in our marriage. We want to give our readers a deeper insight into our lives, and where our story really begins. There are many things our viewers and followers don't necessarily know about us.

Ling

Regardless of what you might think right now what love and well-being is, or what society has told you will bring you happiness and what love looks like in a relationship, we are here to tell you that it's often when you walk away from social norms that you find yourself. We have discovered what it takes to experience true love and happiness. And we can't wait to share that with you in this book.

We both have "the journey to now" stories that reflect what we are most passionate about. While I followed in my father's footsteps by pursuing a modeling and acting career, appearing in TV shows, commercials, and print magazines, Lamb had humble beginnings that led to a music career and starting a reform movement for prisons. We discovered from a young age how important it is to chase after those things that bring you fulfillment, spark your joy, and fuel your passion for loving life — while still giving back.

Sometimes those passions can change into something bigger than you could have ever imagined. My love for entrepreneurship gave me ten years in the real estate industry. Even though I couldn't stand those jobs at the time, I'm still incredibly grateful for the experience I gained because it prepared me for opening a nail salon with Lamb and other entrepreneurial ventures.

It is when I started vlogging that I found joy in sharing my journey with the world. Blogging and becoming an influencer in the process were my creative outlets, which coincided with my passion for being creative and artistic. I aligned my life and career with those things that bring me joy. Marrying Lamb only added to that lifetime of joy and well-being.

Lamb

I have a passion for music. I thoroughly enjoy recording new songs and producing music videos you'll want to watch over and over again. It fills me with joy to travel to perform my music and speak up about the change I want to see in the world.

Scan to hear Lamb's music.

Together, we are not just a married couple but also business partners. We both enjoy content creation, being spontaneous, and showing our viewers the importance of doing so with the one you love. We have learned that happiness is found when you follow your passions, regardless of what life has presented you.

And that joy can be explosive when you work with your partner to achieve success, dreams, and aspirations.

What we are excited to share with our viewers and fans from TikTok, Instagram, YouTube, and Facebook who we lovingly call our Famington, is where we both started out in life. How we grew into the people we are today, and how those steps of success have made our marriage the dynamic it is today.

Granted, we've overcome huge challenges, to include cultural shock and differences. I'm certain that Ling will never get used to dinner for breakfast when I cook her the foods that I am used to making in my country. Or that I'll ever stop learning something new about American culture that will no doubt shock and confuse me. But we do know that the love we have for each other is much deeper than what we see others experiencing.

Ling
Coming together changed our lives forever. While we might have been great individually, it wasn't until we came together that we were able to see just how wonderful our lives could be. This book is how we, Ling and Lamb, step-by intentional step, became this BEAUTIFUL FOOLISHNESS.

An Introduction to Ling & Lamb

Chapter One
A Childhood of Memories

"Too many of us have tried to tone down our weirdness for friends or partners only to later learn that we were suppressing the best things about us. There's no joy like the joy of being your strange self and finding that there are people who love you for it."

— Boze Herrington, author of "The Prophets"

Lamb

I was born in Lagos, Nigeria. A lot of our followers are always confused about whether I am Yoruba or Igbo, which are two different ethnicities in Nigeria. Sometimes, our viewers will comment that I sound more Igbo, while others will describe me more as Yoruba. But the truth is that I am both of them.

I am Yoruba because my dad is Yoruba. But I am also Delta Igbo because that is where my mother is from. To add to the mix, my dad's mother is from a different country in West Africa called Ghana. So, I'm a combination of all these elements.

I was born into a family where my parents were separated at the time. As a baby, I grew up with my mom's family, which consisted of my grandparents and other siblings. While I did not grow up rich, I know that I had an enriching family environment.

We lived in a mud house. Our normal routine in the morning was to wake up and help Grandma. Whatever is going on in the house, you have to help out. At one point, I even used to sell vegetables in the Igando market square.

Ling

I was born in New Jersey to my wonderful parents, Carl and Vernice Holmes. We were only there for a short time because my parents then moved to Norwalk, Connecticut, with the hope of getting away from city life and focusing on starting a family in the suburbs. I was only three years old, and my brother was barely one year old. While I'll always say that I was born in New Jersey, I truly grew up in a relaxed town in Connecticut. There were five of us in total because of my grandmother, Sandi. She was literally like a second mom and was always with us, and even to this day, she's still with us, thankfully.

Growing up, my dad was very successful in acting and modeling. He's always been very creative, and success followed his creativity. He

Ling photographed with her mom, grandmother, and younger brother.

appeared in Super Bowl ads and various print ads and worked with Spike Lee and Denzel Washington.

He was very popular to the point that my friends would always tell me, "I just saw your dad in a commercial," or "I've seen him in a magazine." It was cool seeing and hearing that growing up.

My mom is also super creative. I grew up watching her travel all over and succeed as a really big fashion designer in New York City—not only a fashion designer but also an artist. I feel lucky to have two creative, funky, fashionable parents.

Lamb ———

I would describe my childhood as fantastic because of the community that raised me. My mom and dad always traveled for work, so they were not around as often. It was my siblings, my grandparents, other relatives, me, and the community members. It was one big family.

I remember running around the neighborhood of mud houses wearing nothing but my pants, rolling my tire. No shoes. No shirt. I just enjoyed the feeling of running and playing. While my family was very poor, I was still always happy.

My grandparents were very tough and disciplined. I think I am the person I am today because I grew up with a lot of discipline.

Even though we didn't have money, I had plenty of insight into things and the understanding that life could be tough, but that's okay; I knew this was part of my childhood, and discipline was an important part of survival. My grandma taught me how to cook, and I will always be grateful for everything she taught us kids. I remember that I used to grind our peppers and tomatoes and blend them together on the stone. The movement is something that my hands can still automatically do today. We couldn't afford to pay someone who would blend the peppers and tomatoes, so I hope to teach Ling one day.

All my childhood, I cooked with firewood. You name it, anything and everything—I cooked with firewood. There was no oven or microwave, not even a gas stovetop. We did not have running water, so we would have to fetch water from the well and carry buckets on our heads to fill up the water drums outside our house. Therefore, we never had cold water or a faucet to fill our cups. Neither did we have a fridge.

I'll never forget my first memory of eating chicken and rice. That is because we only ate chicken for very special occasions, like festive seasons such as Christmas. We would only eat rice on Sundays because it was seen as a delicacy. It was a big deal to eat rice. I knew nothing of fancy restaurants until I was in my twenties.

Drinking Coca-Cola back then was seen as a sign of good living. Even apples were a rich man's food. The apples I grew up with are not the same as the ones in America. Anytime I saw someone with an apple growing up, I knew that they were so wealthy. I grew up in a house where I never watched cartoons as a kid. There was no television. I also remember growing up without a bed. Instead, we had sleeping mats. It was sometime later that I had a bed.

Another thing that my family did not do often was take pictures. Ling has shown me pictures of her growing up, like her first birthday. It amazes me how many photos her parents took, and when I see them, I try to picture myself and what my life was like during those captured moments.

Lamb photographed with his older brothers, Feyi and Tunde.

Ling ───

Growing up, my family life was amazing. I am very thankful that I am still very close to my family. My brother is one of my best friends. When we were little, I would set up traps for him, or he would pretend to be my horse. We would play Little Mermaid, and he would be Flounder, the fish, since I was always Ariel.

To this day, I am very close with my mom and my dad. They are also two of my best friends. All four of us have always been very connected, so I grew up with a strong support system, surrounded by love. My parents modeled love, laughter, and silliness, which I brought into my marriage. When my grandmother came to visit, it was the same thing. It was just an extension of that love and silliness I experienced from my parents. I got so excited when my parents announced that my Naa was coming over. It meant great times, cookies, and Seinfeld!

Our home was a hub, all sorts of close friends would come and spend time there. Ladies from church like Mary and Kendrea, as well as other friends of my parents from work, The house was a haven for many, and while my parents would put us kids to bed at night, music could still be heard from the other room because they would have these huge parties. That's probably why I can still fall asleep with the TV on today!

Up until the age of eight, I can describe my childhood as people, parties, and love felt when we all came together. That spilled into the friendships I built within the neighborhood. After school, we would drop our bags off at the steps, and immediately run to meet up with each other at a treehouse, playground, or wherever 'the spot' was for the day. The place at the back of the elementary school was a favorite.

At some point, my mother stopped working full-time. She put a ton of effort into my and my brother's childhood to help us explore our creative side. She was always doing arts and crafts with us or doing baking

Ling around six-years-old.

projects. It was great to have her help us explore our innermost creative selves. I believe this guided my interest in the creative space I find myself in now because I grew up with a glue stick in one hand and construction paper in the other! Growing up, one of my favorite activities was playing with Polly Pockets and my Barbie and Ken dolls. I would get so deep into that world of pretending that if you knocked on my door when I was between a Barbie and Ken scene, I wouldn't know how to react. I would be like, "Wait! You're messing up my entire life right now!". That is how super serious I was because Ken was about to ask Barbie out on a date. I had a serious love for Barbies and the pink Barbie convertible.

Playing with dolls, Tamagotchi's, and having sleepovers where we would gush about all the late 90s and early 2000s music and top bands were my favorite things to do. I could say my childhood was incredible.

Lamb ———————————————————————

At some point, I went to church often. My grandma made sure we kids were involved in church so that we didn't play around in the neighborhood and get into crime and all those other nasty things.
It was because of this that I discovered my passion for music. The leader of the children's program spent time getting to know us kids, and once they found out that I was tilting more towards music as my main interest, it became a part of our church time as well. My interest in music and creating music became very natural because of my involvement with the church.

Lamb photographed with his paternal grandmother, Ama.

Ling

I started modeling because of my dad. When I was younger, around four years old, I was included in pictures with my dad, which were published in magazines or print ads.

I loved doing this with him and always wanted to go with him when he was modeling. From there, I grew up modeling and continued through my young adult life. Soon, modeling turned into acting. I loved watching my dad rehearse his lines, helping him with his blocking scenes, and falling in love with the art of acting. Soon, I was getting commercial jobs for Jell-o and small roles on children's shows such as Barney. It became a part of growing up and exploring my creative side like I had seen my parents do for years.

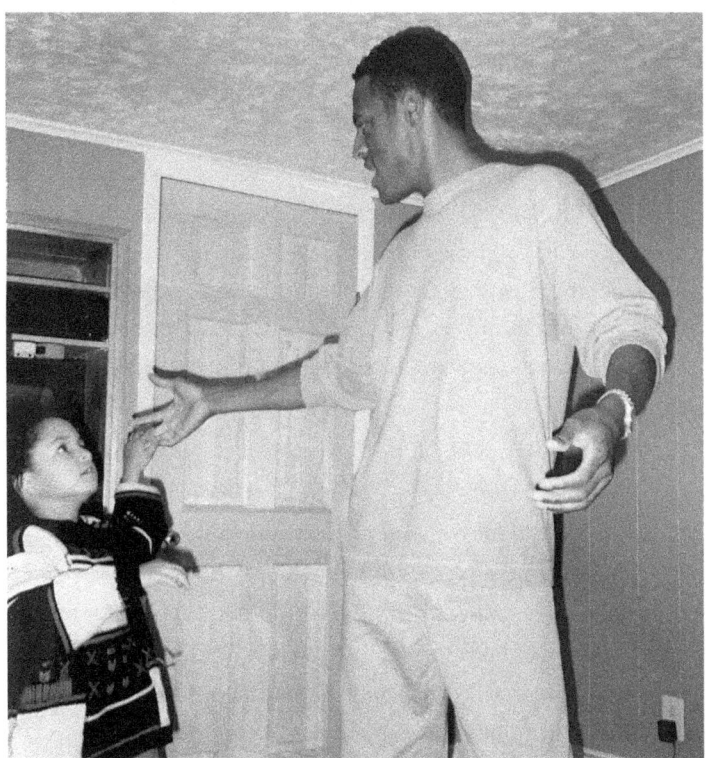

Ling photographed with dad while rehearsing.

Ling photographed with her dad, mom, and brother.

Lamb ───

There came a time when I wanted to take my music globally, and that's how I got into the industry. I experimented a lot with my sound to the point that it became a journey for me. Music is about continually trying to discover yourself or reinvent yourself. Even now, I'm still discovering and working with my sound. It's a continuous journey, and it makes me so happy.

Ling ──

Things really changed for me, and my family around the time that I was nine. My parents took a huge hit financially. While my brother and I were never spoiled, it was easy to see the difference at Christmas when, in the past, there had been tons of toys to open, yet after the financial loss, toys became scarce. We usually had food on the table, but there was a period we went through that I called our "just add water" phase in life. At this point, most of what we ate was cheap and only required adding water to "make it a meal".

As I grew older, things started to look different. I would hear very secretive and serious conversations between my parents. Deep down, I knew something had changed, even if I didn't realize what was happening right away. They struggled financially for a very long time. When I reached the age where I understood what was happening, life became stressful and very, very hard. At one point, we even lived in someone's basement. But all the while, my parents were a strong couple. They worked together and supported each other. The love I felt from them and saw between them never changed. Even in their arguments, they always tried to be very conscious not to argue around us kids and keep the peace as much as possible.

We had each other, and that's what got us through that very tough time. Our support for one another allowed us to survive the situation the best we could. That element has always been in my life and has never changed.

Ling photographed with dad.

Lamb

I'm from a country where there are systems that do not work properly. The judicial and prison systems are broken. There are thousands of men and women who are incarcerated and awaiting trial for a long time, even for minor things like littering or road traffic offenses - prison should not be a place for them! Because of this, I felt like I could use my talent and voice to bring hope to men and women behind bars.

One of the things that a lot of our viewers don't know about me because they never see that side of me is that I was the first Nigerian musician to organize musical therapy concerts in the prisons. This had never happened in the history of Nigeria. I started an initiative in 2009 called "Say No To Crime," then later changed it in 2014 to "I Believe In Africa Initiative."

The initiative led me to perform concerts in the prison. Along with performing, we also cooked and served food to the inmates. At the concerts, sometimes there would be upwards of four thousand inmates.

Lamboginny in KiriKiri Prison, Nigeria for his prison reform concert. (PC:CNN).

There was a big change in my prison reform movement in 2012 when I found out that a lot of inmates were in prison for minor offenses, like littering or road traffic offenses - community service is one thing, but prison was NOT appropriate! They had been awaiting trial for several years. That's when my involvement got serious, and I realized this was far beyond music. I started working with lawyers to get some of these wrongfully incarcerated men and women out of jail.

We started raising money to pay for the bail for these petty offenders. Something I felt at that time, which I still believe in today, is that most of those people were not supposed to be sent to prison. - they were not criminals.

In 2017, I continued working on my prison reform movement for ten years without focusing on anything else. This same major concert at a Nigerian prison caught the attention of other countries and brought me to America for a fundraising concert. We held the "SALT" Album concert in 2017 at the medium-security prison Kirikiri, Lagos, Nigeria. I was able to get CNN, BBC, and so many other news media outlets to cover it. It was the first time in Nigerian history that international or local media was allowed into a prison. During those years, we were able to release 132 inmates from jail. Music literally set them free.

Scan to watch the concert.

It was a lot of work and very draining. I pioneered an original vision that nobody had ever done before in a country of two hundred million people. There were so many silent battles that were fought, and it was very heavy on my shoulders.

Because of the type of family I was raised in, I became a voice for others. All that we achieved took much energy, diplomacy, and advocacy.

Ling

Anyone who knew me growing up, whether friends, friends of the family, or even acquaintances, would always tell my parents that I was very mature for my age. I had a sense of maturity to the point where I felt like I didn't go through a crazy teenage "finding myself" period. I believe that came from a deep knowledge of who I was and what I wanted.

It's never changed. I've always wanted to act and model, which is my conduit to give back to people in other ways. I use our platform today for change and for giving back to the world. That's always been what I wanted to do, and that's why I feel that I didn't go through those turbulent years as a teenager when most don't know what they want to do or who they are.

The most challenging thing I dealt with as a young adult and even into my adult years was watching my family and myself struggle, which was incredibly tough. However, I also had an outstanding balance with my friends and actively went into the city for auditions, acting classes, and seminars. I kept busy by following my passions. It was a creative outlet for me as I developed what was inside of me.

At the age of fifteen, I started working as a babysitter and in retail stores. I didn't get to pursue acting and modeling as actively as I wanted to because, at that point, I knew that I needed to start taking care of myself financially. My mom and dad were struggling to take care of my brother and me, so I knew that I wanted to contribute. I understood that I needed to because we were in that tight spot.

Lamb

During no part of my childhood and even young adult life did I ever dream that I would end up living in America. Even now, after living in America for four years, I am still learning a lot about the people and culture. Once I entered the entertainment industry, I started to understand a few things about America. But nothing compared to what

I know today. The first time I ever left Africa was in 2017, when I went to England to do a show. That was so different from anything I had ever experienced. I had a show in Leicester City, UK, and part of the cultural shock here was the mannerisms of people, the way they speak, and also the food. Also, it was the first time I had seen so many white people in my life. It was also my first time performing inside a prison outside of Nigeria and seeing white inmates at the HMP Prison, Leicester. It was all so new to me.

Even so, it did not prepare me for my first trip to America in 2018. It was a complete cultural shock, one that I am still getting used to today. My shock does make for some pretty great videos, which I am happy that Ling captures. We love to laugh together.

I was a different person until I met my wife. She unlocked the child in me in a way I've never seen before. Now, did that stop me from still touching lives? No. In fact, I still do my social justice work here. Even though people thought I would be too distracted by Ling, she made me enjoy it even more.

Ling

After high school, I kept working and attended as many auditions as I could manage in New York City. Even when I had to wake up at 3 am to make the 5 am call time, I still worked hard to chase after my dream.

There was nothing better than getting a callback and moving forward to the next step in the audition process. That was always encouraging to me when I got great feedback from the director or agent in the room.

Even if I didn't get the job, it was still a good learning experience. Yes, sometimes I would cry because I really wanted these big opportunities, but I was still going to continue with every chance that I got.

This helped me understand different parts of my life when I didn't get something that I originally thought I should receive. Sometimes, the role wasn't the best for me, or truly, another actress was just a better fit for a role. I was able to relate this to all aspects of my life so that I could keep moving forward and not beat myself up. I tried hard to be a responsible adult while trying to live my life. I pursued what made me happy, and I was able to book some cool acting jobs. I was in scenes in the shows CSI, Law and Order, and Thirty Rock. I'll never forget spending three days with Alec Baldwin, Tiny Fey, and Tracy Morgan.

Lamb

This is how I met this fine girl and how this fine girl met me, too.

Scan to watch how Ling & Lamb met.

Ling

When I received Lamb's DM about appearing in his music video, I asked my mom, "Is this the guy you're working with for the concert?" My mom had nothing but praise for Lamboginny, the man from Nigeria with a mission and a beautiful singing voice. I told her I wouldn't do it because I didn't know him and wasn't familiar with his music. If he wasn't Chris Brown or Future, I didn't care.

My mom tried to convince me by explaining how Lamb was a really nice guy. So, I left his request message alone for a few days and eventually came up with a reply. I used the excuse that I was busy with work, but I might be able to take some time off for the music video. It was my way of setting myself up for a cancellation, even though I wasn't busy.

Then, Lamb sent me the music for the video. The day before the shoot, Lamb and his stylist came by my house to review the outfits for the big day. He asked me if I had listened to the song yet, and I had to admit that I hadn't.

Not even the first few seconds to know the beat or a single lyric. Regardless, after speaking to my mom, she convinced me that Lamb was a great person who was doing positive work. Even if I didn't know him as an artist, at least it would look good as an acting credit on my resume. So, I decided to do the video at that point.

During the entire music video process, Lamb was so sweet and timid. He spoke perfect English when he asked afterward, "I would love to stay in touch with you. Can I have your phone number?" Lamb admits that he was trying very hard to be like an American with this attempt at perfect English and to be honest, the effort was cute. I was very sick that day, one of the most horrible stomach aches of my life. Because of this, he offered to take frequent breaks. He even offered to send his assistant to get me ginger ale. (My favorite unofficial stomachache remedy.)

Initially, since I saw my relationship with Lamb as a job (because I've always been a model and an actress), I decided to give him my number. I saw no problem with it from a professional point of view.

Lamb ———————————————————————————

I respected Ling's professionalism. However, when I saved her number in my phone, her name read: *Peace, My Wife*. Even today, her name is still saved in my phone like that because it was prophetic.

I'll never forget the night that Ling called to tell me she was in love with me. In fact, she had admitted to her parents. I was so shocked that I wrestled with my blankets to sit up as my heart was ripped apart. The happiness that filled me caused me to cry right there and then. It was one of the most memorable moments in my life.

From the day I met Ling, it was like putting the last piece of a puzzle together. Everything has been made clear. The joy I feel now with Ling is ten times greater than the happiness I felt before. But that is the truth of the matter. While my life with Ling was filled with silliness and love, we both took the time to learn what made us happy before we met. Unlocking that happiness in your life is what we both believe is the key to a lifetime of laughter with a partner.

There is nothing like family. I've lost my mom, my dad, and my grandparents on both sides. I lost my dad on the 1st of June in 2009, and 18 months later, I lost my grandma. My grandma was my baby. Losing both of them in a short period of time was hard.

When I first saw Ling, I immediately saw her as my family. The fact that she was able to unlock a part of me that I didn't even realize was there is a part of our wonderful shenanigans, which the whole world gets to enjoy today.

Share Your Thoughts

What are some childhood moments that shaped your life?

It's crazy to think that the things you experienced in your early childhood life could significantly impact some of your patterns today.

When you reflect on your past, you can see why you do some of the things you do today. A deep understanding of that helps you see yourself in a new light.

We will ask you to share your thoughts throughout the book; this is an introduction to this activity, which you can participate in at the end of each chapter.

**Loving Yourselves Enhances
Your Love For Each Other**

Chapter Two

The Power of Self-Care

"It's not selfish to love yourself, take care of yourself, and to make your happiness a priority. It's necessary."

— Mandy Hale, *author of "You Are Enough"*

Ling

Before we were an official couple, we both had experienced what it was like to end a relationship that wasn't a good fit for us. Not that these previous relationships were terrible, but there comes a time in every failed relationship when one or both people can feel that the relationship is no longer growing. Ending the relationship is the only logical way to find contentment and love again. There are huge benefits of being very natural and rational when discussing the end of a relationship. You'll be so relieved when you end a relationship you've realized doesn't align with your ideals.

Lamb

When my previous girlfriend and I mutually ended the relationship, it was a no-brainer because we realized we were not a good fit. I used the wisdom of understanding to step out of that relationship. I knew it was not going to work out. You have to be able to critically look at a situation to make the best decision.

Instead, I started to focus solely on my passions. I dove head first into creating my album, which sparked a lot of inspiration. These interests led to the biggest concert ever in the history of any prison in Africa that I performed. A promoter reached out to me to start doing concerts outside of Africa.

Because of this energy I built by focusing on my passions, I was later invited to the United States for a concert. You know how the story goes from there.

One of the biggest life lessons I learned and implemented into my life is giving myself time to heal. After I came out of that relationship, and having experienced deep heartbreak in the past, I understood that the time had come to recover from all past relationships. I needed to take the time to have clarity about my future and to prepare my heart to experience love in all its forms. It was that decision that led me to the relationship I have with Ling today.

> "Unlock your happiness by making the right decision by not lying to yourself." -Lamb

Ling

I had a similar experience to Lamb's in a previous relationship. When I ended the relationship with an ex-boyfriend, I realized that the relationship was not the right fit for me. I accepted that even though the relationship had failed, I was not a failure.

I struggled with the break-up because all my friends were married at that point in my life. I felt the pressure of needing to be in a relationship, so I tried to make it work. But I knew it wouldn't happen based on how I was feeling. I had to make a big decision.

Simply put, I knew that I deserved better. It's important to know that you will never ask for too much in a relationship with the right person. You should be getting back all the good things you put into a relationship. Realizing this helped me make the big decision to end the relationship that wasn't a good fit.

This break-up helped me gain the confidence to move on. I was now in a place where I could say, "Okay, it's just me. Now I need to focus on what makes me happy." I was going to enjoy my happiness while being single. I focused my time on learning more about myself and becoming self-aware of the things and activities that brought fulfillment into my life. As a naturally introverted person, I never had issues spending time alone. Yes, at this point, I had to get to the bottom of understanding, "What do I really like to do?" One of the exercises I used to discover this well-being can be found at the end of this chapter in the "self-care plan" section. I spent time traveling to different places around the world and hanging out with really cool strangers. I had great experiences as I challenged myself by getting out of my comfort zone and discovering the activities I enjoy. When I got back into the routine of doing those things more often,

I discovered true happiness, even without having a boyfriend in my life. A few years after I started on the journey of personal joy, Lamb came into my life. I was only focused on what makes me happy and on being a good person. I let God take care of the rest. That's the only way I can explain it because nothing else makes sense as to the exact moment Lamb entered my life at the right time.

One of the most beautiful lessons I learned from this experience is that good things come when you are not looking. I wasn't worried about the next relationship as I focused on my passions. Instead, I let God decide when the right relationship would come to me.

There is a lot of value in life that has nothing to do with material things. When we were preparing to be married, we did not do what most couples in America do today.

We did not have a big wedding. There were only ten people present when we were married in my parent's living room on January 4th, 2019. I bought a dress that was about $100, and we got a nice suit outfit for Lamb at H&M.

After the wedding ceremony, we went to a local historic estate, Gallaher Mansion, Cranberry Park, to take pictures because it was absolutely STUNNING, and it helped that it was free of charge! It was a beautiful park with a castle-like estate in the background.

When people saw our wedding photos, they thought we had been married at that estate. But we just had a very simple wedding that didn't cost thousands of dollars. I don't even think it came to $1,000, LOL!!!

My parents gave us some money after the wedding so we could spend two nights at a hotel in Danbury, which was only forty minutes from where we were living. It wasn't anything over the top for our honeymoon, but it was magical. It was snowing outside, and the landscape was absolutely beautiful. We had each other, so everything was beautiful.

Lamb

What made it so special was a completely stress-free wedding. We didn't have any disagreements about the wedding. That is how we would recommend anyone get married. Too many times, we speak to people who complain about how much they spent on their wedding, and they complimented us because they agreed we kept our wedding so simple.

Ling

Our wedding was more intimate than what most couples experience, as it was attended only by a few close family members and friends who are like family in my parents' tiny living room. After the wedding, we didn't owe any debt because there were no fees to pay for a caterer or venue. Our simple wedding made it easier for us to enter our marriage stress-free. We didn't worry about starting a new marriage with debt from the wedding. We didn't let the societal standard of what a wedding should be like control what we felt was good for us. Our love was more significant than the material aspect of the wedding. The actual ceremony of it all is what we value.

Now, as we look back on that simple wedding, we agree that we wouldn't have it any other way. Even if we could have afforded a big, lavish wedding, we wouldn't do it. Our wedding day was immensely special and unique to us because it symbolized our real, tangible love for one another. That is something we would never want to change. No matter how our circumstances might have been different back then, we would always redo our wedding the way it happened.

Lamb

I will admit that I didn't know much about self-care routines until I married Ling. I wasn't prepared for what she would teach me. Yes, I did make sure that my house was clean and that I cooked for myself. But I was always so focused on what needed to be done that I never really spent any time for myself. I never practiced self care.

I never felt settled when we lived in that small room at Ling's parents' house. In my head, I told myself not to get comfortable, as I only focused on, "How can I get my family out of this?"

Ling

He was determined not to have time for a mud mask. He thought that he didn't deserve it.

Lamb

She started forcing those things on me. But I will tell you right now, she did a great job. She would come and just love me, even in that situation. She would do the self-care for me as she taught me all the ways I could just stop, focus on myself, and make sure that I was good.

Hair. Face treatments. Exercising regularly. Massages. Meditating. She introduced me to all of it. Personally, I had never done these things before because I had never thought about it. While we were living at Ling's parent's house, I didn't often come out of the room. I remember her mom calling Ling at work asking if I was okay because I never came out of the room. I didn't want them to think that I thought this house was mine. So, I was only focused on getting us into our own place.

It wasn't until we had our first place together that I started taking my self-care routines seriously. But it all started at the beginning of our marriage when Ling loved me so much that she was willing to teach me about different ways to just take time for myself, recharge my batteries, and be the best version of myself so I could be there for others.

For me, I learned that food is my self-care. In moderation, of course.

Today, I still don't need Ling to tell me to respect her because I see how she carries herself. I see the way she respects herself. There is no room in this relationship for either of us to treat each other less. Even in our toughest arguments, we don't cross certain lines. That is because we genuinely lived this process that you are reading in this book. Love is bigger than any argument.

Ling

I volunteered at the local farmer's market for one year. Every Wednesday, they would organize a farmer's market for underprivileged members of the community. Anyone could come to the farmer's market that day to get all these amazing foods and veggies for a reduced cost. Being a part of that was the best feeling in the world. Sometimes, these people would talk to me with tears in their eyes as they shared their stories, and it gave me such a fulfilling experience to know that I was helping them. No matter how big or small.

Sometimes, the reason why people stay unhappy is because they never take action. It is easy to read this chapter and think about all the things you can do to spark joy in your life — things you will use to create your own self-care routines — but it is another thing to actually do it. So, as you are reading through this book, prepare to take action. If you don't take action, you'll never be able to change the life you are living right now.

Lamb

I always felt that personal hygiene, or lack thereof it, could become baggage. So, I worked on myself. I always took care of myself in the best way that I could. I will never forget the time when my friend's wife called me, begging me to talk to him because he had been wearing the same boxers for a week. It was crazy how he let himself go. I would never do that to Ling or myself. This goes to show why self-care is so important because one day, you'll have people relying on you for this type of advice. You must put self-care into practice, not only for your future but also for the future of your family.

Ling

I definitely didn't stop my self-care routines after I married Lamb. I always take time to work out multiple times a week. I always have time in the morning for my skincare routine. I have 'wash my hair' days. Sometimes, I just go out and do my own thing or run errands because it makes me feel good. It makes me feel healthy. I feel happier. And I am a better person for Lamb and others around me.

What Our "Me Time" Looks Like

Lamb

I love to take morning walks near our local park. I also love making calls back home to stay connected to close friends and family. It makes me feel like I'm "there" without actually being there. I stay in touch with my board back in Nigeria for my organization, Saving. All. Lives. Together (S.A.L.T.).

Of course, I *LOVE* food as part of my self-care. I didn't have an expansive palette back in Nigeria, so coming here and trying all of the amazing foods I've tried so far is definitely something I like doing for myself.

One of the top things I love is working on new music. I record at least 1-2 songs a week. Music is my therapy and creative release. If you give me a mic, I'll create magic.

Ling

My "me time" is going to the beach at sunrise - even on days when it's raining and there is no sun; I just love the beach. The sound of the water, the stillness that's there before the rest of the world is awake. Here, I can be present in the moment.

My self-care is working out. I love riding the Peloton and doing Pilates. You can always find me doing some new Nyansh (Lamb's nickname for booty) workout. I also love modeling and acting. Anytime I'm on a set, I'm in my happy place. To relax and express myself, I love to read and write. It's something I've been good at since I was a child. I've consistently scored highest on those writing and reading tests in school, which is why I was successful in my blogging days. I've always been very creative, which I attribute to my parents.

My daily and weekly routines focus on my skin and hair care. I feel strongly that when people look good, it will help them to feel amazing as well. How we feel about ourselves is exactly what people around us will pick up on.

Lamb

The bottom line is this — take care of yourself! You can't expect to take care of anyone else in your life until you take care of yourself. I cook, as you may know, and that's because I've always been trained to cook for myself. My grandmother taught all the boys in the family how to cook because she said, "Just in case your wife is in a situation and can't cook in the future, who's going to cook for you?" She wanted to make sure that we could cook for ourselves. That's how she raised all of us to cook every day.

Even before I met Ling, I washed my dishes. I cleaned my house. I cooked. I wanted to continue these good habits when we got married. My wife is not my slave. She is not my house help.

I continue my good self-care habits so that we can help each other.

I think that the opposite of self-care and doing those things for your mental health can lead to things like frustration and depression. You're constantly looking for approval from the people around you. You're looking for validation. That's when you fall into the 'see me' syndrome trap.

This leads to never being content with the blessings around you. That is why it is vital to be aware of your needs and how your self-care routine can fulfill them—like your need to feel happiness, joy, and love in your daily life.

There are consequences of not having any self-care routine or habits. You need at least one hour daily to attend to yourself. That is a real game-changer.

Ling

I also feel that everybody should have at least an hour for themselves, even if it's thirty minutes in the earlier part of the day and then thirty minutes at the end of the day, or one consecutive hour. Something that allows you to take that breather, or whatever that hour looks like for you to relax and decompress.

There are twenty-four hours in a day. You should, at least, have that one hour for yourself. Even if you don't do anything it's a time to recharge your batteries.

Lamb

I'm learning to relax because of Ling. In the early days of our marriage, my head was always thinking. In my culture, we are always on the go. Literally, when I was young if I was sitting around, just relaxing, my grandma or parents would say, "You're just wasting away like that."

It wasn't until I was older and married that I learned, with the help of

Ling's guidance, that I wasn't wasting time. It is a well-needed time to recharge. I'm learning to shut things down, including my mind. Sometimes, I catch myself still all over the place when I'm just sitting down. So, I'm still learning to truly shut it all down.

Chapter Two: Key Takeaways

- No matter what you decide to do for your morning and evening self-care routines, the bottom line is that you are doing something for your well-being.

- When you feel good mentally, physically, and spiritually, it will be tangible on the outside and visible to others.

- When you know yourself to the fullest extent, then you'll be prepared to enter into a romantic relationship, knowing what you can and cannot accept.

- Don't stop reminding yourself who you are and what you are worth.

Share Your Thoughts

How are you going to spend your daily hour of self-care?

In this writing exercise, list how you want to spend your own hour. Make a plan. Will you break up your own hour for thirty minutes in the morning and then another thirty minutes in the evening? Or are you going to use your one hour all at once?

Your self-care plan might look something like this:

- Morning walks on the beach.
- Morning facial routine.
- Time dedicated to a hearty breakfast and dinner.
- Turning off your phone, computer, and all electronic devices for one hour.
- Journaling for thirty minutes.
- Praying and meditating.
- Reading a personal development book and taking notes for one hour.
- 30-minute exercise class / yoga in the afternoons or mornings.
- 30-minute coffee break with sound - reducing headphones on while you listen to music.

_____

_____

_____

_____

_____

_____

Embracing the Journey ─────────────

Chapter Three

Fulfilling Our Destiny

"The purpose of life is to live it, to taste experience to the utmost, to reach out eagerly and without fear for newer and richer experience."

— Eleanor Roosevelt, first lady of the United States from 1933 to 1945

Ling

I support every single musical effort that Lamb puts into all his songs. Anything that he has in his mind that he wants to do, I like to verbally affirm, validate, and support him. Even during those times when he was recording music in the closet because it was the only place to capture good audio when we were still living with my parents, I would still record him. I wanted to remember those moments because I knew there would one day come a time when he would be recording in top-of-the-line studios.

I wanted us to remember this part of our lives and be able to treasure just how far Lamb has come with his music.

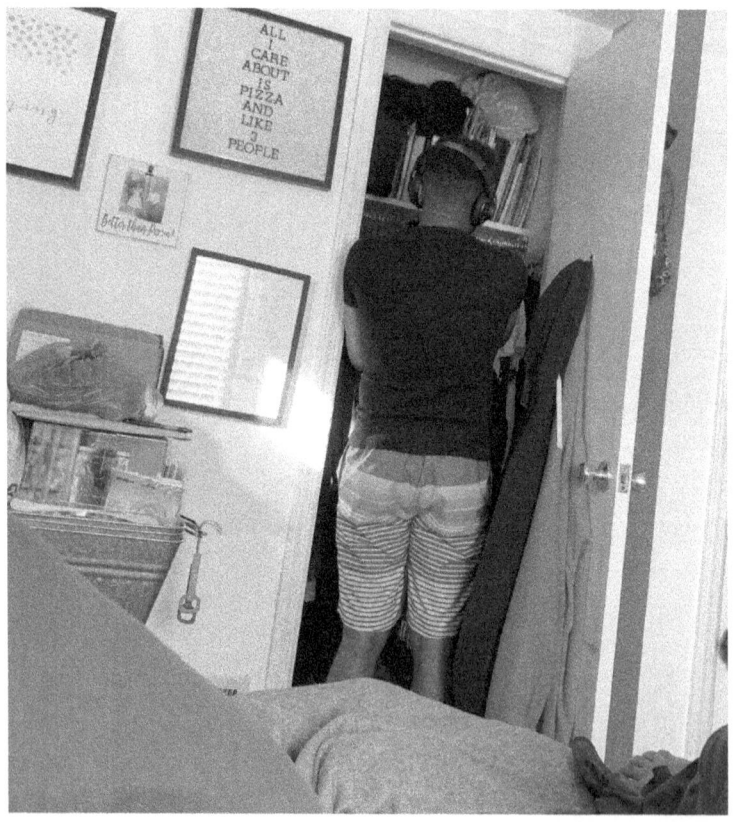

Lamb recording his songs in the closet.

There were times when Lamb would feel down and out, but he was still pursuing what made him happy in hopes that it would finalize in the way he now sees it. He wanted to get signed and go on world tours and other things like that.

For me, my support of his passion started with little encouragement, like, "One day, it'll be bigger than this. It'll be better than this. But you're so amazing for doing it, even in the closet."

That's what it looks like to get behind your partner. Even if I don't know anything about music, I'm still going to support Lamb. I used to sing in musicals for theater, but I don't know any of the technicalities about recording music. I don't know how hard it is in the sense that I know what it's like from an acting perspective to try out for a role and not get it. But I don't know what it's like to work for years just to get a manager to represent your song in hopes it will get played on the radio. There's so much that goes into it.

I just want to make sure that I'm there for him. I'm able to do that because there is balance. I can still turn around and do what makes me passionate and still be there for him. I think you can do both as long as you're aware enough to know that somebody else needs you too. It takes a lot to push yourself. So you need to have something left to be able to push another person who you care about.

Lamb ───

Supporting my Bambi (our pet name for each other) is a no-brainer. I remember one of the very first things I did when we started dating was that I went to her blog and read everything from the beginning. I literally went through the entire blog. At that point, it had been a few years' worth of posts.

For me, that is when I found out that I cared about her beyond just romantic love. I remember that I had discovered that her Instagram page was not properly linked to the blog. Right there, I felt like a winner for noticing!

I told her that the blog was not functioning correctly. She was pretty surprised that I found it because she had no idea. That's how I started genuinely looking out for her.

A few days after the music video, I had invited Ling to a park to get to know one another. As an actress and model, I knew she was really into pictures. So, when I saw the perfect picture with her as the silhouette against the sun, I asked her to let me capture it. I then remember telling her that I would take photography classes to help out and take her best pictures possible.

Ling
I was sitting there thinking, "WHAT?!!" I wasn't interested in him yet. We weren't even dating. This was a couple of days after the music video, and all I could think was, What is he saying? He's leaving in a few days. What does he mean he's going to take photography classes?

Lamb
For me, I believed she was already going to be my wife. But, her perspective was closer to - he's going to get on a plane back to Africa! I saw a future vision of our life together. I didn't feel any form of competition in terms of defining my support for Ling and her passions. I knew I could do both: continue my music and support Ling. I was already thinking that if I married her, she would become a part of me. The same way that I wake up and plan for my music or my prison reform project — she became a part of my plan.

I began dedicating time to everything that was important to me. Looking back on our relationship, I have taken some of the best pictures she has. I always try my best.

Another good example is from a few weeks ago. I talked to Ling about taking more pictures. I told her, "Don't sleep on your modeling. I think every week you should try and see if you can do a photoshoot." It might not be a big one, but I knew it would help her to get back into that space. The way I saw it, the more she practiced modeling, the more creative she became. And the more I photographed her, the more creative I became.

It's not stopping my music. It's not affecting my career. It's not affecting my prison reform. It's not even affecting our vision together.

You have to understand that we each have an individual vision that we constantly remind each other to keep. We keep supporting each other on our individual journeys and what we now have together. When it comes to the Ling and Lamb brand and our marriage, we are in this together.

She has never come to me to say that my melody is no good. She allows me to be my professional self while doing my music.

Ling

I'll give him feedback, just like he gives me feedback. I always try to be constructive, but what Lamb does with that feedback is his own choice. We always help each other out in that way.

Some might say it's easy for us because we're both in the same industry: entertainment. You might be thinking, "Well, what about my spouse? He's a real estate agent, and I'm a hairstylist." My answer is that you two can still come together and support each other.

A couple whose passions and careers are in two different fields can still align together. The husband might check in on the wife to see how things are going, and her response might be that things have slowed down with her clientele. Even though he knows nothing about her field, he can still support her by suggesting that she can further her education or ask if there are any classes she is interested in, like cool new highlight techniques.

She can do the same by asking how his sales have been lately. "Have you sold the house you've been talking about?" If he answers, "No, not really," she could suggest some ideas and tactics. "Are you dressing up the house inside? Do you want me to come make it look pretty?" This shows that the couple is willing to come together and support each other, even in opposite careers.

There is always a way to come together and support one another. It's about loving that person you have partnered with. You want to know them and support them while receiving that support, from them. It's a balance.

Lamb

Individually, we have destinies that must be fulfilled. Getting married should not kill an individual's destiny. Rather, getting married should align with a destiny. This is what I call destiny alignment. What I discovered about my beauty, and me, is that our destiny aligned when we came together. This helps us to achieve that individual purpose.

If Ling has been destined to be a billionaire, I shouldn't get in the way of that. It might be that she takes one viral picture, and BOOM, she becomes a billionaire. Who am I to get in that way of her purpose and destiny?

This is key because I've seen a lot of people get married and, literally, just die. They're alive, but their destiny just dies. Marriage should enhance your destiny, not the other way around. Instead, you are elevated by the support of your partner, and vice versa.

My biggest motivation was watching Ling take on the family challenge of paying all the bills and purchasing our food in the early stages of our marriage. My motivation increased when I found out the cost of the food

I was eating - because I like food a lot.

That realization locked me in on the family goal. That goal became making sure that business was good and that together, we could generate multiple sources of income. I'm making sure that the financial trust she has placed in me is forever intact.

I say this jokingly to Ling often because I mean it. I tell her that my goal is, "Even if I fall and die tomorrow morning, I will make sure that you are not hungry. I will make sure that you have money to take care of yourself." I know she doesn't like me saying this, but that is how she knows this isn't kids' play and that I truly love her and will take care of her.

It's a strong, intentional way of thinking. When you genuinely love yourself, this is how you begin to think about your future and the future of those you care about.

We weren't sure how it would all play out when we took these steps to achieve our goals together. We were hoping for an expected result, and we both knew we had to put a plan into action.

Ling

When I was working as a property manager for a residential apartment complex, people would come back from work and pass by the office on their way to their apartments. And when they'd pass by, a lot of times for whatever reason, my desk became the therapy desk.

"Oh, what a day," I would always hear. Everybody would be in suits, and I would know their salaries and how much money they make. And all I could think to myself, who was making $20 an hour (much less than what they were making)? What are you complaining about!?

What was going on was that none of them were happy doing what they were doing. They were lawyers their dad wanted them to be or doctors their mom wanted them to be. They all had careers that would bring them money but weren't happy.

It was because they weren't following their passions. It was often because they feared their passions wouldn't bring the money.

At some point, you have to decide how to balance both making money and following your passions. It's all about finding a way to make your passions bring you money. Some might think it's silly because they don't equate what makes them happy to dollars.

But when you write it down, you can sometimes surprise yourself. "Oh, wow! Maybe I can start this business. Maybe I can see if this is popular enough, and I can get into it. Maybe there is money in this and something that will help me feel fulfilled."

I know someone who wasn't happy at all but made great money. They took the time to write down the things that they liked and eventually narrowed it down to I like helping people manage/understand money. Now, they are trying to figure out what that journey looks like to translate that statement of happiness into income.

Once you write it down, you can start figuring it out and go from there.

Lamb

The older I get, the more I understand that being an adult comes with a lot of responsibility. That was the first reality check I needed to understand that, as a human being, things may go in two places.

It's either your passion and what you are destined to do that is provided for you to be able to meet up with that responsibility as an adult — or you have something else, like getting a job on the side to show responsibility.

Now, lucky for you if you can meet that responsibility through what you're passionate about. But if it is something you are not passionate about, yet it helps you meet your responsibility, then you have saved 50-70% of a headache. Hey, you have money. You have shelter. You have clothes.

Look for that activity that you are passionate about. While you might feel that you've missed the opportunity to do it professionally, like a professional sport, you can still do that thing that brings you joy and fulfillment. You might not have made it to the big leagues, but look for a club where you can play that sport once a week. It still makes you feel good to play in those types of tournaments. You did not lose out on the chance to have fun with that activity.

When my music wasn't doing any form of numbers or success, even though that is what I am passionate about, the reality as an adult is that it wasn't paying any of the bills. What did I do? I started volunteering with the YMCA in Stamford and kept looking for jobs there. I finally got an offer at the Y and Lowes but had to choose Lowes as I could walk there because we didn't have a car. Although I wanted to work at the Y, Lowe's was the more responsible choice. I went out there and got a job, which enabled me to support my family.

The days I wasn't working, I was trying to record music. I didn't let it die because I had a job. I always look for a bit of time when I go for my morning walk, where I will record melodies. Then I'll send it to my producer.

Even now (I have to be honest with you, Famington), my music is not paying any of the bills. The reality is that I'm doing what needs to be done in terms of work to make sure that I always take care of our family. Because of my hard work and commitment to responsibilities, I can now pursue my music on a big scale, and that's when my music will start blowing up.

It's great to see streams growing with my music. I'm putting a band together now. I'm shooting music videos. I can do all those things because I took care of my adult responsibilities.

Ling

We both took responsibility in the sense that when I was vlogging as my hobby and creative outlet, I didn't quit my job and say, "Okay, people make money blogging. I'm just gonna do that." Instead, I decided that until it makes money, I'm going to work because I still have to pay bills. Vlogging as a hobby helped me narrow down that it was something that I liked to do. At the end of a stressful day, it was so lovely to do something I enjoyed.

Lamb

Both of us did not quit our jobs at the same time. I quit because I was injured while doing my job. For me at the time, it didn't make sense for me to keep going because it could have led to a huge medical issue. I was going to doctor's appointments, which would have cost more money than I was making.

Thankfully, at that time, our side hustle, content creating, was making more money. We had just completed a big job, which made enough money that I didn't have to continue working. Ling was slowly able to quit her job as well. Finally, our passion started making money, allowing both of us to quit our jobs.

Ling

Some people just made the jump and quit their jobs after getting just a few viral videos on TikTok. Even when we had hundreds and then millions of views, we still kept our jobs. We can't understand why anyone would quit their job to try and create content full-time. Not until it starts paying all the bills 100%.

Lamb

Our content led to different jobs. And then we got an agency. That is how we knew that it was time to pursue our passions full-time. If you are not careful, your passion will take you on a journey you cannot recover from.

Ling
Because if not, you'll go broke.

Lamb

If uncontrolled, your passion can take you to a lost destination.

Ling

I wanted to quit my job much earlier. I wanted to quit about seven months before I did because I was just so done doing what didn't fulfill me. I have a lot of faith, so when I see something, I just know it will come true. I knew in my heart that we would start booking jobs, so I didn't need to keep working at a job I didn't want to be at anymore.

Lamb was the voice of reason. He encouraged me to sit tight until the other jobs that I wanted to be doing were secured. We waited until we reached a point where we would be okay if I quit my job and another job didn't come for the rest of the year. We had to make that decision first before taking that calculated risk.

Lamb

I tell you this one hundred percent: every human has more than one passion. But if you refuse to acknowledge or check within what you are passionate about, you'll only end up going after one passion. Go back and look inside of you. Look at yourself again. What makes you happy?

Chapter Three: Key Takeaways

- The more time you spend doing the thing you are passionate about, the more creative you can become.

- A couple whose passions and careers are in two totally different fields can still come together and support one another.

- Getting married should align with your destiny. This is what we call destiny alignment.

- It's a strong, intentional way of thinking. When you genuinely love yourself, this is how you begin to think about your future and the future of those you care about.

- Eventually, you must decide how to balance making money and following your passions.

Share Your Thoughts

What does it take to achieve your passion?

Learning and Unlearning ─────────

Chapter Four

It's a Lifetime Journey, Not A One Night Stand

"Being a student is easy. Learning requires actual work."

— William Crawford, American politician and judge during the early 19th century

Lamb

You used to look at me like a lunatic.

Ling

Well, yeah. I still do... For Lamb, breakfast can include chicken, rice, sauce, and plantains. It's like, "What are you talking about?!" Breakfast is waffles, pancakes, sausage, scrambled eggs, and bacon. That's breakfast. Lamb gets up in the morning and makes his chicken, sauce, rice, and plantains. He'll jokingly say, "You're just going to have to deal with it."

The funny part is that after all these years together, when I wake up, I'll ask him, "Are you making the rice?" It's a little bit of unlearning for me what breakfast should look like every morning. I still definitely love my pancakes and bacon, but the only thing different I had eaten for breakfast before I was with Lamb might have been a slice of cold pizza after a crazy party. I had to unlearn that typical breakfast foods were not the only thing you can have for breakfast.

Lamb

Now she likes chicken with rice for breakfast.

Ling

Well, I still have my champion way, which is pancakes, bacon, and scrambled eggs. But I am accepting and open to the fact that you can do dinner for breakfast.

Lamb

That's right. You can have my type of breakfast in the morning, and then you are ready for the next twenty hours of the whole day. The moment you decide that you want to bring someone else into your life as a partner, you must be willing to learn, unlearn, and relearn. You are coming from a world that was built outside of your partner. Your partner also comes from a world built outside of you. Then, both of you come together and need to start afresh.

You're going to start building together from scratch. Yes, Ling learned to accept my type of breakfast, and I learned to enjoy pancakes, scrambled eggs, and orange juice.

Ling ———————————————————————————————
And sometimes he asks for American breakfasts, and it's the cutest thing ever.

Lamb ———————————————————————————————
That's right. Sometimes, I have to hustle Ling to make pancakes, "You promised that you were gonna make pancakes." But the point I'm making is that it's important for me not to get stuck in what I know and never to be willing to try things the way Ling does and vice versa.

Ling ———————————————————————————————
You can't go through life or enter into a relationship thinking you have everything figured out. You're going to learn that there are many things about your partner that are different in the sense that you might have different morning routines, prefer different foods, and tackle challenges in a different process. Life is all about learning and pivoting in order to experience happiness and love with yourself and in a healthy relationship.

I was never saving for a house individually, nor was Lamb. Honestly, before we were married, we weren't really great with money. Lamb always gave his money to charities and his music. For me, I could see five homeless people in a mile radius and instantly become broke because of giving to each one along the way. Or I support my family members before taking care of myself.

But now that we are together, we are focused on our savings. Lamb has learned a lot about finances, especially here, in America, because it's a totally different system. We have an entire video that covers me trying to convince Lamb to open his first credit card so he could build his credit score. He was very much against the idea, and it took a lot of convincing for him to agree.

Scan to watch the video.

Lamb ──

I fought getting a credit card. Where I come from, it's cash or nothing. I saw it as a trap for me in my head. "Why am I buying a phone if I cannot afford it? Why would anyone buy anything they can't afford right there and then?"

Thanks to her, her dad, and my friend, who is a banker, we talked about it. Then I understood that it's not even about if you have the money. This country is built because you need a particular credit score regardless of having a million dollars in the bank. I learned that there was no point wasting money on buying things with more expensive interest rates because the system isn't going to trust you.

That's why I opened up my first credit card and started building that trust. In 2024, it is just amazing where my credit score is. That is something that I had to learn and accept.

When you find yourself in a particular position in life, the first thing you should always do is, regardless of what you have read or studied in the past, look at the situation itself and identify what it requires to solve it. It might be nothing that you know or know how to fix, but then you have to learn what it takes to change things.

That is why many people go to school, graduate, and then come out into the field and don't know what to do. What they've read in the textbook is different from the reality of life. It's theoretical versus practical.

Ling

Lamb now has learned the importance of financial literacy and education. He has really done so well and has even become friends with bankers, so he has a really good understanding. He has the knowledge to take care of himself and our family financially, which is great. I think it comes with the maturity of being in a relationship.

Don't get me wrong. I'm sure there are single people who are probably saving for a home. It just wasn't us before we were in a committed relationship. That was our goal when we came together. Both of us have always wanted to be entrepreneurs. I always knew that I wanted my own cosmetic or beauty line.

Lamb

For me, I've always been very "charity-minded." But it wasn't until I came to America and was married that I developed a business mindset. I found a good balance of being both charitable but also smart with my money.

Ling

I watched that before my eyes. He has a great balance of giving back and helping but also making sure he keeps his new financial goals. He has a way to keep himself together financially for himself and his family.

Lamb

I think what made it easy for me is that I watched Ling literally take care of us when I had no job. I had no money. In my head, for the very first time in my life, I stepped out of the charity world that I have always been in and started thinking, How do I make sure that my wife is never in a position to look for money, for food, shelter, and basic needs?

Once she explained the credit system to me, I thought: How do we ensure we are forever good? It's no longer about me but about us together as a family. That led to me obtaining financial wisdom.

Finances *almost* affected us in our marriage. Sometimes because of the traditional upbringing, people feel that certain things may be forbidden in their tradition or cultural belief. You must also understand at that point that the happiness of your home is greater than your cultural beliefs, and find a balance quickly. You must also unlearn or figure out a way to accommodate your partner's beliefs and traditions.

That is why you start on a clean slate when you both come together. You and your partner both begin to contribute to that fresh beginning a marriage gives you.

At the beginning of our marriage, we argued and went back and forth. We're not anywhere close to that now because of that journey of learning to understand each other. Now if she tells me she doesn't want to eat my fish pepper soup, I don't look at her crazy.

Scan to watch the video.

Ling

Oh, no. I can't I will never try fish pepper soup again. But that was just a part of my learning because I knew that it meant a lot to him. I know Lamb had to do a lot of unlearning when it came to his ties to food. There were times when he'd make traditional dishes that I didn't want to try or eat. He takes it personally and gets offended.

For me, it was just food. I was honest with him and explained that no one should tie that much emotion behind food. If I'm saying that I actually don't like it or it makes me sick, then I'm not going to try it or force myself to eat it just because it's Lamb's traditional food. There are a lot of American foods that, to this day, Lamb has not and will not try (we may or may not still be working on it, LOL). Cheese pizza Mac-n-cheese, he won't do it. It breaks my heart. Pizza is my favorite food. I literally have a tattoo of pizza. I love pizza, and he won't do it, which is ok because I still love him anyway, and honestly, more pizza for me! Lamb had to learn that it's okay that I don't like all of his food because it doesn't change my love for him. I love him a million times over.

Lamb

I used to feel very offended when she didn't like my food. It was something that we originally fought about at the beginning of our marriage. What I learned is that Ling's love for me doesn't associate with whether or not she will try my traditional dishes. And it was the same with me. While I might not like pizza, I still love Ling very much.

One of the things that helped this chapter of our lives is that Ling doesn't eat spice. At all. Therefore, what joy is it going to bring me that the woman that I am in love with experiences any form of medical crisis or pain just because she was trying to please my culture?

When we fell in love, I didn't present a list of all the cultural foods in front of her that she must eat and like before we were married. There was nothing like that for either one of us. While we are both foodies, we fell in love with each other's personalities.

It is key for people to always go back to the foundation. How did we get here? We didn't get here because of the food. We didn't get here because of the language. We got here because we both deeply love each other.

Ling

Because he was sooo cute.

Accepting each other without the desire to change one another is one of the key aspects of our relationship that contributes to our daily joy. I've never tried to change Lamb from who he is.

One of the best things about Lamb to me is his accent. I love the words he uses that don't necessarily mean what I mean—or they do, but they sound more dramatic. The only times I will correct him, and if you've watched our content, you've seen me do it, are when he legitimately says a word incorrectly. I don't want him to get around someone else and say it, which might cause them to think a certain way about him.

I will educate them in those ways, but otherwise, his accent is something I don't want him to ever lose. I don't want him to lose all the things that make him exactly who he is. I encourage it. I love when he's on the phone with someone back home because I never want him to lose that connection to his past life. I don't want him to lose the cultural way he is because it makes him who he is, and it makes him so unique to me. I might tease him sometimes or just try to help educate Lamb, but that's never me wanting to change him. It's very much a way we "poke at each other" and have fun while learning at the same time.

Lamb

I will be very fair to Ling's side. Whenever she has tried to correct me or teach me how to pronounce a word, I know she is just trying to ensure that people can understand me. This is America. The fact of the matter is that a lot of the times, they don't understand some of what I say.

We went to the grocery store once, and I was trying to ask someone where the "bo-ger-ba" was. Two grown men were looking at me for a good five minutes. They were like, "What are you saying?"

Ling

I'm just giggling in the back because I don't want to help him when he's trying to do his own thing. He really wanted to do it on his own and have that experience.

Lamb

So, I say again, "Where is the buga? The bugaba." They were just looking at me. So, I had to start describing. "You put the bread here, and the bread here, and there is a meat patty in the middle between buns." Finally, they asked, "Oh! Do you mean BURGER?!" "Yes, I mean bURgER." I had to use an accent just to enunciate the 'r's!

Ling

If you lost your accent and became Americanized - which sometimes people do when they migrate here and they want to assimilate, they want to be like regular Americans - I would be so sad. I could have just married an American at that point.

Our dynamic is a lot like the show I Love Lucy, where Lucy tries to understand her Cuban husband, Ricky, and his accent. "What do you mean 'splain'?" she'll ask when Ricky is saying "explain." Our dynamic is pretty much like that every day. That's why Lamb says it's our love language.

Lamb

This is how we learn from each other. Personally, I can enjoy it when she is trying to correct me and she is trying to sound like me. It also helps when I hear myself speak. "What do you mean buga?" You know, it's just fun and part of the learning and unlearning.

Where I come from, we pray very loudly and aggressively as if we want to fight with God right before us. I was used to that method of prayer. Then here Ling is, silent as the word. At the beginning of our marriage, I used to not feel comfortable. I used to ask her to pray louder because I wanted to hear her pray, and she would say no. That wasn't her way of praying.

But this is where the "unlearning" or acclimating came from. God never wrote down a specific instruction on how to communicate with Him. So, each person has their own form and ways of communicating with Him. When I understood that, I immediately unlearned my expectations.

I didn't unlearn it for me because I still pray like that. For me, it's like God is right in front of me, and it makes me feel good. But I did unlearn the expectation that Ling had to be the same way.

In this process of learning and unlearning, what people need to really understand is unlearning the expectations of others. People expect and are used to certain ways, but instead, it is better to unlearn expectations so that people can flourish in their ways of communication. At the end of the day, the most important thing about prayer is that a message was passed along.

When we first got married, we received a lot of comments from Nigerians on social media saying that Ling should already know how to speak my language, Yoruba or Igbo. People wanted to know how much of the language LIng knew and if she could cook all of my favorite dishes. Is she? She should. She. She. She. She. She. Please leave her alone! was all I was thinking. People expected Ling to totally assimilate to my culture and leave hers behind.

I didn't marry a cook. I didn't marry a servant. Ling is my partner. She is somebody who is half of me in everything that I do. This is important: learn to be patient with each other in learning each other's culture, mannerisms, language(s), and dishes.

There are people who looked at us after one year of marriage and had expected us to rush everything. This is my response to that – if it takes my wife twenty years, so be it! We are not in a hurry. Our marriage is a lifetime journey.

Ling ───

Every marriage is different, and not every marriage will face the same cultural differences as Lamb and I have experienced. But for every relationship and marriage of the same culture, there is still plenty of learning and unlearning a couple will experience. That is because you and your partner are still coming together to make it work with different habits and routines the two of you are already used to. That is why being fully transparent with your partner before marriage is so important.

Chapter Four: Key Takeaways

- You are coming from a world that was built outside of your partner. Your partner also comes from a world built outside of you. Then, both of you come together. You will need to start afresh.

- When you find yourself in a particular position in life, the first thing you should always do is, regardless of what you have read or studied in the past, look at the situation itself and identify what it requires to solve it

- The happiness of your home is bigger than your cultural beliefs. You must find a balance quickly. You must also unlearn or figure out a way to accommodate your partner's beliefs and traditions.

- It is key for people to always return to the foundation. How did we get here? We didn't get here because of the food or the language. We got here because we both deeply love each other.

- Accepting each other without the desire to change one another is one of the key aspects of our relationship that contributes to our daily joy.

Share Your Thoughts

What do you need to learn or unlearn?

Possible undesired effects can happen when sticking to your own perspective, culture, or expectations of others. Instead, it's important to be willing to be flexible, open-minded and have the ability to drop all expectations. One of the biggest issues that couples have is holding onto unfulfilled expectations of their partner.

So, what do you need to learn or unlearn about yourself and your partner? Write it out and share it with them.

_____

_____

_____

_____

_____

_____

_____

_____

_____

_____

_____

_____

_____

Communication with Your Partner

Chapter Five

Keeping It REAL

"Words are singularly the most powerful force available to humanity. We can choose to use their force constructively with words of encouragement, or destructively using words of despair. Words have energy and power with the ability to help, to heal, to hinder, to hurt, to harm, to humiliate and to humble."

— Yehuda Berg, international speaker and best-selling author

Ling
It was pretty tough, but at some point, I knew I had to tell Lamb about my debt. I remember it was November 2018 when I said, "Okay, I need to tell you something. I know we've been going out and doing things, and you know how I like to pay for things, but I want you to know that I don't really have as much money as it might seem. Most of these things are on credit cards." It had become a situation where I was stealing from Peter to pay Paul.

Lamb
Robbing Paul to pay the village is more like it!

Ling
That was it. So, I had to have this discussion with Lamb to explain, "As much as I really want you to enjoy yourself, this doesn't mean you're not going to eat," because I told him from the very beginning there would always be food, I don't care what the case is. We need to tone down our spending a little bit and decide what we want to do and if we can afford it because I'm running low."

Lamb
That's when she came clean about it all. The debt, the total amount owed, and everything.

Ling
While Lamb understood what debt was, credit card debt was completely new to him. I explained that my debt was tens of thousands of dollars, and it felt like I was utterly drowning at that point. I just wanted to be honest with Lamb, admitting that I didn't know when I would be able to pay it off and that I'd been working on it for years. This was my reality. I wanted him to know this before we went any further in our relationship—before we were even engaged, at an early stage in our dating. The fact of the matter was that I wanted the person I would

be with to know as much about me as possible so they could make an informed decision about whether this relationship was what they wanted.

I was transparent about everything, not just money. This specific instance was a big deal. Unfortunately, I fear that many people sweep it underneath the rug and wait until they are married to think, Well, my spouse isn't going anywhere now. I'll tell them about the debt piling up on me. Then, that debt becomes the other person's responsibility, whether they like it or not.

I didn't want my debt to be a surprise for Lamb (even though I do enjoy surprising him). After that discussion, he told me how much he appreciated me being honest and open about my finances.

Lamb
I certainly trusted Ling more because of her honesty. I then knew what I was dealing with going into this profound relationship. The part that scared me (even though I'm sure I haven't told Ling this part) was the amount. I was still getting used to converting everything in American dollars back to my Nigerian currency.

For things that were only $10 or $20, I would do the math and have a mini-panic attack. "That is too much!" I would say. So, you can only imagine how I felt when I figured out the amount of Ling's debt in Nigerian currency. Wow. Tens of thousands of dollars....this is where we're going to start from.

When your partner opens up and becomes transparent with you, it is NOT for you to weaponize it against them. It is for you to understand it and figure out how the two of you will come out of it.

When Ling told me about the amount of her debt, I first told myself, Do not weaponize this information against her. It was for me to be aware of and then understand how we can both climb out of it. The moment we both started making money, it was our priority to clear that debt and definitely do so before we started thinking about purchasing a house.

Over time, as we both focused on that priority, Ling also became better with money. There was a point when she got a raise by changing her job and received a bigger salary. But I told her, "Even though you have a bigger salary now, still act like you are still getting your old salary. Whatever is extra with your new salary, begin to save it." And that's exactly what my wife did.

So, that transparency helped me understand how quickly you can get into debt in America. But it also allowed me to help her escape that seemingly never-ending pit of misery.

Ling

Being transparent isn't always about money. You should be transparent about many things with your partner before committing to a serious relationship. It's important to begin sharing everything with your partner to avoid a potential disaster.

You should be transparent about:

- *Children. Do you want them? If so, how many? Couples who get married and only later share that the wife wants children, yet the husband does not is a failure in communication and can result in many issues, even divorce.*

- *Sex. Yes, sex. Talk to your partner about what you like and don't like, and make sure you learn your partner's preferences, too. If your partner likes something you are unwilling to do, that could become a huge issue later on. Sex is a major aspect of a healthy, loving relationship and not an issue*

Scan to watch the video.

that should be taken lightly. This topic can make or break relationships.

- *Do you plan to work after marriage or become a stay-at-home parent? Be clear about your picture of what marriage looks like to you, and learn your partner's idea of marriage.*

- *Strengths and weaknesses: Let your partner know if you are not a good cook or that you hate doing the dishes. If you and your partner don't like cooking, who will cook? What is the solution there? See how you and your partner can rely on each other's strengths to compensate for those weaknesses.*

- *Your life goals. Be honest with your partner about what you are trying to accomplish.*

You want a partner who can support you, and who you want to help towards their own goals.

Lamb

I've always been grateful that I was transparent with Ling from the very beginning. Unfortunately, when you look at where I come from, Nigeria, many times, people won't trust Nigerians. They think we only want to scam you or start some other drama.

Keeping it transparent is important to us. Whenever I told her who I was, she knew it was exactly what she got. I never told her details about myself that she couldn't prove was true. When we got together and became serious, she then saw traces of who I was not - compared to the stereotypes of Nigerians. She knew that I was a musician, but not what society thought Nigerians were.

I know married people who still don't know what their spouse does for a living. They don't know what their partner does all day. I remember asking a person once...

"What does your husband do?"
"Oh, he's a businessman."
"What kind of business?" I ask.
"Oh... it's... uhhh. He's just a businessman."

I'm forever grateful that I didn't feel like I had to lie to Ling. She trusted me because she knew she could fact-check if she wanted to do so by looking at my social media. Even now with the success of our Ling and Lamb brand, people still send DMs with pictures of me in the newspaper from so long ago. So, if I was lying that I was a musician, she could have easily found out.

I can hear her now. "Ummmm, why is there no history or trace? You said you did all this prison work and all that, and no one knows anything?". Even today, followers will send Ling things from my past on the internet and bring them to my attention, yet I have completely forgotten about them. She'll see my old videos and photos, and we'll crack up over it.

While we're laughing, all I can think is WOOOOOW. If I was lying to this woman, it would have been a problem. I am so grateful I never said I was someone I wasn't. This is true transparency.

And she kept it real with me, too. She never told me that she was someone that she wasn't. She told me that she was an introvert and didn't have too many friends. Honesty is beautiful like that. Being completely open with each other and accepting one another for who we are is absolutely beautiful.

Ling

If you have expectations of someone without first letting that person know, you're only going to set yourself up for failure, major disappointment, and ultimate misery. It's like thinking, Why does he never wash the dishes after I cooked dinner? And then getting upset when that expectation was never communicated to your partner in the first place. Your partner might be relaxing on the couch because he thought you liked cooking and cleaning. You're upset and mad, while he is fine.

This is what happens when there is no communication in a relationship. Your expectations of yourself or your partner should be discussed upfront and thoroughly.

That example is similar to what Lamb and I experienced earlier on in our marriage because I did have the expectation that if I cooked, Lamb should clean up after dinner, and the other way around. If Lamb cooked dinner, then I would be in the kitchen cleaning. But what happened is that when I saw Lamb cooking, he was cleaning as well.

It would have been wrong for me to expect Lamb to clean up after I'm done cooking when he's used to doing both. So, we had to communicate that expectation so we were both on the same page moving forward.

Lamb

The way I was raised, while you are cooking you are cleaning. That way, by the time you're done cooking, you don't have so much mess around you. When we were living with Ling's parents, I remember noticing how Ling's mom would cook and then Ling would do the cleaning. While I didn't see this as an expectation of what Ling would expect from me in the future, it was the perspective that this is how they do it in her family.

Today, when I cook any meal, I clean up after myself as I go. That is ingrained in me. But I also know how Ling was raised, so I will help out in the kitchen when she is cooking and make sure the kitchen isn't a mess when we are done. This is how we do this one thing in our home because we shared about how we were raised.

Expectations can be dangerous. When you expect your partner to do something or be a particular person, and they're not, then you'll only be miserable. Instead, build your expectations around your love and respect for each other.

We have never said to one another, "Oh, you are the one that is gonna clean the house tomorrow." No, we just carry the vacuum around, and we're vacuuming. It could be me, it could be her. Sometimes if she leaves dishes in the sink for too long, I will tell her, "Ah, you've left this dish for too long. I'm just going to clean it." I don't mind. But you know, she always does the laundry.

Ling
That's right, I just take care of it. It's not because he's like, "Well, you do it." No, it's because I really don't mind it.

Lamb
I think you enjoy it. Because you do it so well that I don't even understand.

Ling
Actually, I hate it. I don't trust him with the laundry. Here's the transparency, Famington; I don't trust him to separate the colors from the whites. The delicates from the rough, sturdy towels.

Lamb
A good example is that I did the laundry the other day.

Ling
That's right, and he let it sit in there for 24 hours! And it stunk and had that funky moldy smell. Now he had to re-wash it all over again, and it was backing up washing my own laundry. It's funny because he just sat downstairs with this sad look on his face.

Lamb

And I'm not sure if she caught the fact that (and I don't even know why I did this) I had my white shirt in with colored clothes and now it's blue.

Ling

This goes to show that when you have an expectation, you have to come together first with your partner to talk about it and figure out what works for your relationship. While I rely on Lamb's great cooking, he relies on me to clean our clothes.

Lamb

Every marriage is different. I repeat — every marriage is different. There is no blueprint. Some women were raised to cook, clean, do laundry, do everything, etc. They can get married, and it works for them to continue doing those things.

Other women are raised in a home where they see their father and mother helping each other. That is the mentality they come into a serious relationship with. Some are raised who never cooked, cleaned, or did laundry because they had someone to do it for them.

According to how you were raised, it is important to communicate your background genuinely to your partner. This ensures that your partner doesn't have unnecessary expectations of you. This is how communication and transparency help to shape the expectations of your own home.

Ling

Even if it's something small, it's still very important to communicate your habits and tendencies. I told Lamb right from the beginning that I am not a morning person. I don't even talk till after 10:30 AM. Don't bother me until then!

Lamb
While I start talking at 5 AM.

Ling
Therefore, it was important for me to let him know my morning tendencies so he could understand why at 7 AM. I looked like I wanted to punch him in the face. Now, he knows not to get caught off guard if he tries to wake me before 10:30, and why I look so angry if he does. Instead, he can wait until I'm ready to take on the day and be my "normal" self.

Lamb
For me, I love to cook. But there are times when I have to request that Ling cooks because I'm not eating out again.

Ling
And that's fine with me because it helps me realize that it's probably been a month since I've tried cooking anything

Lamb
I appreciate when Ling cooks her unique dishes, like when she makes mashed potatoes with shrimp and sauce. Forget it. I'm gone. Even though I know cooking is not her favorite thing to do, eating her food makes me so happy. And that's why I think she does it, it's another way to show love.

Ling
It does make me happy the way he loves my food.

Lamb
Mashed Potatoes and Shrimp day is a special day in our house. When she makes this sauce I will eat it with rice, with bread, with anything. And it all ties back to communication. Even though I know she does not like to

cook when she does, it's easy for her to see just how happy I am so she can still have some fun with it.

Marriage is not for kids, what I mean by kids is people who are not mature. Understanding expectations allows you to see your partner and their values in the relationship. When I hear someone say they want to marry a woman who can cook, I tell them, "Good luck trying to find a woman who can always cook AND genuinely love you!" This is what I mean by understanding expectations. At the end of the day, it is about love and not what the other person can do for you.

I look at Ling from the angle of my biggest expectation - not cooking, not cleaning, or anything else, rather is she keeping her morals? That's my biggest expectation for her. We have both vowed to care for and be there for each other.

You can be the best cook and the best cleaner in the world as a spouse, but if your morals and discipline are zero, the whole marriage will crash at the end of the day. That is what I hold dearly in regards to expectations in a marriage. Everything else can be worked on.

If your spouse doesn't know how to cook, you can cook today and buy tomorrow. If God blesses you and you become rich, you can hire a cook. This thing doesn't matter compared to integrity and discipline. That is what protects our legacy as a family. So for me, it's the highest form of expectation.

All other expectations can be planned and discussed with your partner. For example, if you and your partner plan to have kids, plan who is going to handle feeding the children, washing them, clothing them, and taking them to school. It's important to share responsibilities and be a part of that family dynamic while maintaining a healthy sense of flexibility.

Communication is the foundation for creating a team with your partner. It is teamwork that makes marriages thrive!

Chapter Five: Key Takeaways

- Build expectations around the love and respect you have for each other.

- When your partner opens up and becomes transparent with you, it is not for you to weaponize it against them. It is for you to understand it and figure out how the two of you work with that information.

- Being transparent isn't always about money, necessarily. There are many things you should be transparent with your partner before you commit to a serious relationship.

- If you have expectations of someone without first letting that person know, you're only going to set yourself up for failure, major disappointment, and ultimate misery.

- According to how you were raised, it is important to communicate your background genuinely to your partner. This ensures that your partner doesn't have unnecessary expectations of you, and how communication and
transparency help.

Share Your Thoughts

What expectations do you have for your partner? For yourself?

Together We Thrive Achieving More as One

Chapter Six

Teamwork Makes The Dream Work

"Teamwork is the ability to work together toward a common vision. The ability to direct individual accomplishments toward organizational objectives. It is the fuel that allows common people to attain uncommon results."

— Andrew Carnegie, Scottish-American industrialist and philanthropist

Ling

It was in the summer of 2021 that Lamb and I experienced a great sense of gratitude for the presence we had created online. So much so that we decided we also wanted to have a presence in our community. The goal was to have an actual brick-and-mortar setup. It was exciting to think about different ideas that would be tangible for people to come and visit in order to have a piece of Ling and Lamb offline.

We had to think about what that would look like for us. Since we're so heavily into food, we first considered going into the restaurant business. Unfortunately, the logistics of that idea at that time, just did not make sense. Also, with it being the height of the COVID-19 pandemic and many restaurants were closing down, we decided that wasn't going to work at this point in time.

So, we had to think about another business idea that wouldn't make our online business take a hit. When the perfect business idea manifested, it was as though the stars had aligned, and God said, "Here it is!!" It happened at the perfect time and we could both work together to get it started.

People always comment on my nails and how much they love them. I even get stopped at the grocery store or by strangers on the street who ask me where I get my nails done. It was because of multiple instances like these that we opened our own nail salon. We knew then that it was time for us to finally go into business with a physical location.

A space became available immediately after we started looking for ideal locations, and we were both very surprised because it was all coming together very quickly. We both had to make decisions and agree as a team who would handle the logistics of opening the salon. I started designing the space and ordering supplies, while Lamb had a very tough task of his own.

Lamb

While we were working together to open a physical business, we also moved homes. While I relied on and trusted Ling with many aspects of setting up the salon, she relied equally on me to put our new home together. With the setup of the salon on her plate, she told me, "I don't want to have anything to do with how you design our new house that we're moving into! It's totally up to you — I trust you."

Ling put her faith in me to design our new home. However, I still took her shopping with me to look at different pieces of furniture that would fit our unique new space. Even though the task was mainly mine to complete, I still included her with my design ideas.

We really agreed as a team to open a nail salon, and then we delegated the different tasks we had to complete to make it a reality while in the process of moving from one home to another. By communicating with one another and relying on each other's strengths, we accomplished many things. While we both agreed on the nail salon business, I will admit that it wasn't my world. Ling is the one who had more experience getting her nails done, and what she knew would be a good experience for our clients. I trusted her as my business partner and my partner in life. I was still there because I could move chairs around, and I'm very proud of the chandelier I picked out for the space. But those were my main contributions.

This shows that you can still be a team player, even if you're not sharing the project equally. While she was at the nail salon every other day overseeing the construction and planning the purchasing of all the supplies so they would arrive in time, I made sure our new home was put together. She still communicated with me every part of the salon's design process, and I ensured that I included her in the design of the home as well.

One of the most important parts of working together as a team during this time in our marriage is how she communicated when designing and running the nail salon had become too much. I listened clearly to her because that's what being a team player is all about.

Ling

Even though I was picking out the colors for the nail salon, which turned into the prettiest shades of pink, I would still ask Lamb what he thought. If he had any suggestions, I listened. The same thing he did for me when designing our home. At the end of the day, it was my home, too, and Lamb did a great job of including me in decisions, even if he was the one focused mainly on the design.

Lamb

I think many couples don't even trust their partner to know their passions or dreams. But I say to those couples, "Let your partner know your thinking." Ask your partner about their passions, and then let them create those. Give them the freedom to follow the how and do it how they want. Champion their expertise and not your own opinion.

That is what I did with the salon. I did not say that it needs to be this or that color. Not at all. That is because I *know* my wife. She is a beautiful woman who likes beautiful things. I knew that the nail salon would not be ugly. She made it beautiful, like a candy store anyone could come to. That's why Ling called it "The Candy Shop of Nail Salons"! When your partner knows that you trust them, it builds confidence in them to give the best output.

Although the nail salon didn't thrive, it was an invaluable learning experience that really taught us about the ins and outs of running a brick-and-mortar business. That chapter also opened up new opportunities, giving us more time to focus on and strengthen our online presence—this shift has brought us closer to our long-term goals and closer as a couple.

With our Ling and Lamb platform, we receive all sorts of endorsements that we have to work together on to make decisions. These different companies want us to advertise their products on our platform. When these jobs come in, we have to put our heads together to make sure we can come up with the best concepts for these sponsorships.

Ling ─────────────────────────────

When we are offered brand deals from Crocs, Walmart, and Amazon, we must first send the company a concept of how we plan to include their product or service in one of our videos. It takes a lot of creative thinking because the majority of our content is spontaneous and organic. Even when I plan pranks on Lamb and we are editing those spur-of-the-moment videos, we find ways to include the brand deals we've agreed to. When ideating and creating, we throw ideas at the wall to see which will stick. Then we move on from there. But it always requires us to talk through our ideas together so we can figure out which one is the best idea. I'll admit, sometimes that's hard because we're two different people with two different brains! I'll think my idea was fabulous, and he'll feel the same thing about his idea.

When those situations happen, it's all about putting our egos aside and really looking at what's best for the brand at that moment, whether it was his idea or mine. We decide which idea will result in the most engagement and the most return from our followers. That takes a lot of thinking; that's a big part of teamwork for us. Letting go of your ego to decide what's best is the secret to really making the dream work with your partner!

Lamb ─────────────────────────────

The brand often comes back with their own input. This goes to show that sometimes a team works in three ways. When we send what we think, the brand will come back with something else, and eventually, we'll land on a final idea. In the end, It always works out that we are happy as a team, the brand is pleased as a client, and the viewers are happy with what we put together.

Ling ─────────────────────────────

Through working as a team, we've learned to prioritize by triage: we look ahead at our week to see what we have coming up and what deadlines are approaching, then decide what projects can wait and how to prioritize.

My biggest piece of advice is to employ a calendar, even if one part of your team doesn't like the calendar. It's going to prove to be extremely helpful.

Lamb
Yeah rrrrrrrrright.

Ling
I'm still trying to get him into calendaring. That is key to prioritizing so as not forget things. But even though he might not be the best at keeping a calendar, he still looks at the calendar (sometimes) I've put together to make sure things don't escape our memory. It's great that we have this teamwork because sometimes he goes and reads it to remind ME of upcoming deadlines and what we have going on. (I love when he reminds me - the calendar queen.)

Lamb
The moment you leave your parents' house and agree to become one with somebody. They automatically become your first priority. The way I look at it, Ling and I are all we have. We've been through tough times when we didn't have much money but did have each other. While it might be easy to use something like a calendar to prioritize the things that need to get done by a certain date, it is also important to plan time for you and your partner.

You and your partner can deliberate ideas and plan to take action towards those things you both are trying to accomplish.

It is impossible to go through life all on your own. You will need help from others. When you get married, you are now in a tight relationship with your best friend. Who better to help you, support you, and cheer you on as you chase after your passions? Whether we have a spouse or not, having people in our lives to support us is vital.

You have a destiny to follow, and so does your partner. Together, you work as a team to fulfill those destinies without getting in each other's way. Teamwork is what makes a marriage work. And that is our main priority. To be there for one another, always.

Prioritizing your marriage shapes everything about you. It shapes your career, your friends, and your family. When people, including family and close friends, ask me for money, before I give anything away, I will make sure that my wife is okay with it. I make sure that our bills are sorted, and then, whatever extra is left over, I play around with it. Before, when asked for money, I gave it freely, without worrying about my own finances. I'm telling Ling everrrrryyyything! Guess what?

She says, "Omg, you don't need to tell me everything."

Ling
Ha! If It's ten dollars, I don't care.

Lamb
But you know what? I still say it because she is my priority. The continued happiness of our marriage is our main priority. I don't want to ever find myself not sharing with her. It's easy for me to accept that she doesn't need to know everything, but I refuse to listen to this because if I don't share everything and then make an impactful decision without her – that would be a terrible mistake!

The life and home I've created with Ling is my first priority. If something is not okay, then I am focused on fixing what the problem may be. I won't make an outsider happy and not prioritize the most important person in my life. Even when she's not there, I prioritize my dignity and my character, and I make sure that I do not involve myself in anything that can damage or bring any form of embarrassment to our home.

If I am on a work call and she calls me, I will tell who I am speaking with to hold for a quick moment so I can talk to my wife. I'll ask her if it is important and if not, I promise to call her back as soon as I am done. But I never ignore her call.

Ling

Being a good team player is not something that happens some of the time. It must happen all of the time. For example, if we get into a heated argument, I address things immediately. I want us to communicate in the moment so it's all fresh. I don't want us to remember a different version of something later on. This form of communication is how we work as a team to resolve conflict.

Every argument may not happen like this for you. You may be too upset and just want to run out of the house. I will admit that I have experienced the need to just go out for a drive and decompress after the quarrel is settled. Even though there have been times when I can't stand him, and I don't want to look at his adorable face, I will still call him after an hour or two and ask him what he wants for dinner.

No matter how bad the argument is, I still care about Lamb. I'm not going to let our team down even though there was a disagreement. The same thing can happen in the workplace. You might disagree with one of your co-workers during a work meeting, but that doesn't mean you'll let your team suffer just because of an argument. The same applies to marriage.

Lamb

We have never found ourselves arguing over life-threatening situations. We've never argued about situations that would break our marriage. For example, there is no cheating going on, neither of us has blown our family's savings, and I pray that we never find ourselves in that situation.

In the first year of our marriage, when we did disagree, I always wanted to walk away in the middle of it. Even when we were in the car, and it was moving, I would tell her to pull over and that I was done. But Ling showed me that by talking about the situation instead of letting it continue, we could work as a team to resolve our issues.

Gradually, I learned that if we start an argument, it is important to finish the argument by speaking openly about our feelings and thoughts on the topic. We might disagree, but we still love one another. Even after an argument, I will still make sure she is not cold when she goes to bed. Even if it's one o'clock in the morning, I will make sure she is well and warm. It was just an argument. Not the end of the world.

Ling

Teams are often made up of multiple players. So even in your own team within your marriage, it is still okay to get third-party help. Sometimes, your team is dealing with way too much for the two of you to resolve on your own. Seeking professional help, assistance, and an outside perspective is absolutely normal, not a scar on you as a person or couple.

Lamb

Our teamwork is so strong that I can gratefully say that we have never gotten into a heated argument beyond our control. Neither one of us has ever moved out of the house for a couple of days or weeks. We've never separated for more than a few hours. If we have an argument before 11 AM, it's more than likely that I'll get a pancake to the face instead of on my plate! But that's it. We're soon back to being our silly selves and loving one another.

While I can't give you advice if your partner has cheated on you, I can say that the best thing for you in those types of situations is to seek help.

I told Ling not two days ago that I am trying to get to a point in my life where nothing bothers me anymore. It's not because I don't care; instead, I've come to understand that anger and all those emotions truly don't solve anything. I'm trying to get to the point where if we have a misunderstanding, I just want to talk to her. I want to discuss with her why this situation happened without having to shout those words.

This is my heart's desire. I see myself achieving it already because of understanding the true concept of our marriage and our genuine love for one another. There is this ideology that every couple must have misunderstandings or that if you're not fighting, it's not real love. That's a lie.

You can master a good way of respectfully working with your partner to resolve disagreements. That is by being deeply in love with each other. For me, that is what I'm working on. To reach that level where even if she does something or I do something, I can work with Ling in a way and speak to her that will not escalate the situation. It all ties back to the importance of communication.

Chapter Six: Key Takeaways

- You can still be a team player, even if you're not sharing a project equally.

- When your partner knows that you trust them, it builds confidence in them to give the best outputs.

- Learn to prioritize by triaging every situation and event. Look ahead at your week to see what is coming up and what deadlines are approaching. Then prioritize.

- The moment you leave your parent's house, you agree to become one with somebody. This person automatically becomes your first priority.

- Being a good team player needs consistency.

Share Your Thoughts

What do you feel needs to be prioritized in your relationship?

Master The Art of Waiting ───────

Chapter Seven

The Application of Patience

"How to be successful in life? Patience. Patience. Patience. Patience. Patience. Patience. Patience. Patience. Patience. Patience. Patience."

— Lamb

Lamb

When God created and distributed patience, Ling was busy getting pizza. I can hear him now, "Where's Ling?...Oh, she's at a pizza shop and missed it."

Ling

Yes, I was probably getting pizza that day. I know that patience is essential, and it's something that I probably have none of. Being married to someone like Lamb from a different culture is interesting because even though he was raised speaking English, sometimes I don't understand why he doesn't know what I am saying. There are days when I will say something, and he'll look at me and say, "What? Huh?" This confuses me because I usually respond, "What do you mean? I'm speaking English?" "But you are talking too fast!" he'll explain. "Are you kidding me right now?"

It's this thing that happens all the time when I am trying to talk to him. Other times, it's when he says a word that may not have the same meaning as I think it has, which gets confusing.

I'm the type of person who will say something once, and if you don't hear me, I will say, "I know you heard something, so try to piece the rest together," or, "You have to try to assume what I said because I'm not repeating it."

I'm in a committed relationship with someone who needs explaining multiple times. This tests me daily, and I am working on patience. There are times when I just give up. Lamb won't understand what I said or what I mean, and I lose my patience and just walk out of the room. I have taken the time to process it. I know he speaks and understands English, but it's not his first language. I will never be able to put myself in that place and truly understand because English is my first language. So, I tell myself to take a deep breath, maybe speak louder, and not speak "as fast" so that he can understand what I am saying. When I do this, I realize it isn't so hard. But I must keep reminding myself of this because it's not my nature. I'm not patient. Whereas he's the absolute poster boy of patience. This adorable face right here is next to the word patience in the dictionary. I'm trying to be like Lamb (#BeLikeLamb).

Lamb

Because of how I grew up, I understand patience from a very, very deep perspective. Even though I felt that I had a good understanding of patience, when I met Ling, I had to learn its *application*. I did this by not misinterpreting her lack of patience as rudeness.

She is swift when I ask a question and wants me to figure it out on my own. She'll say, "You have to figure it out," or "Google it." Of course, that's not the answer anyone wants to hear from their partner. But the truth is that I understand her nature. I have to go deeper with my level of patience. By doing so, this helped our journey as a couple.

Each marriage has a unique love language. The more I learned about Ling's impatient nature, the more I understood that I could not bring any story about other people's marriages and how they do things into our home. I needed to truly understand Ling's pace and the best way to deal with her responses when she did not understand me or I did not understand her.

I'm very patient with my wife on all levels. People will say, "Oh, I could never marry a woman who cannot cook or does not like to cook." Even on our social media platforms, when Ling is being silly, and we are playing (like the pranks), some people will comment, "Oh, if it were me, I would divorce her." Every time I see one of these comments, I just laugh because, deep down, I want to teach these people about patience and genuine love.

From our perspective, patience means looking beyond the subject matter. I never lose sight of my wife's overall value. I've never allowed a particular topic or situation (whether it's her impatience or a prank) to convince me to place some level of judgment over her or to try to tell her "no." That is how I apply patience with her.

Even when she is cooking, I am patient with her. She doesn't like cooking, which everyone now knows. People don't understand that it is possible that a woman or a guy would not like to cook. This is how I am patient with her. Have I gone months without her cooking? Yes. But did that change my happiness? No. This is also because Ling was transparent with me in the dating phase about her dislike for cooking, so I knew what I had agreed to about my future wife.

This is the application of patience instead of just having an understanding of patience.

Ling ———————————————————————————————

Patience is something you either have naturally or don't. And you can always become more patient. Naturally, I just don't have patience. So, I have had to learn to get there. I like to think that Lamb's patience is rubbing off on me.

Sometimes, people think patience is a sign of love. Yes, I love Lamb with everything in me. Every fiber and part of my being I love him with. Even though I am not the most patient person, this is not a measure of my love for him. It's a fact that I'm now trying to make myself better and become more patient. That's a journey for me.

Lamb ———————————————————————————————

And she's doing amazing at becoming a more patient person. What you can learn by being patient is that you can recognize the level of patience and tolerance your partner has. You'll not notice this about your partner after just one day. Every love has its own language.

Ling's level of patience from when we first met and started dating to when we got married is completely night and day. When we first got together, she had zero patience. She often told me to "just Google it," and then the conversation would end.

Now, she tries to explain things to me. She walks me through it and ensures that I understand either what she is trying to tell me or how I am using an English word in the wrong way. She still sometimes asks me to "Google it" because that is her nature. But more often than not, she will help me learn and understand. For me, that is a big deal.

Ling
Lamb learned that I'm not getting frustrated with him when I tell him to "Google it" or "figure it out," but that this is the way I like to teach. Often, there is impatience behind my responses, but I also want Lamb to learn and sometimes figure things out on his own.

Lamb
I struggled with it initially because I'm used to being raised by my grandparents, who pampered and spoiled me.

Ling
Yes! Exactly! That's why I always tell him to "figure it out." And sometimes, I do call him a brat. He's such a brat.

Lamb
And that is why I call her sharp mouth. I went from being raised by grandparents who spoiled me and always told me the answer to things to being in a relationship with someone who wanted me to "figure it out" on my own. She did empower me, but I sure didn't like it.

From the beginning, Ling was very upfront with me, saying that she did not like to cook. For the longest time, I would cook, or we would order takeout. But after some time, she started to cook the things that were easier for her or that she knew I loved. Now she cooks not just to feed us but to bring joy and happiness to our home and my belly.

When we married, many people tried to tell me to teach Ling how to make Nigerian dishes. I told them, "No!" I would be patient with her and not rush trying to teach her my language, traditional meals, and all of those things.

But this is what I did. I never told Ling that she needed to go and cook us a meal. Instead, I simply watched and paid attention to her when she would come around while I was cooking. She will look at me when I put this and that into the pan. She watches how I do things.

This reminded me of my grandmother and how she never directly taught us children how to cook. We only knew everything we knew because we were hanging out around her when she was cooking. We'd watch how she was cooking and what ingredients she used. So, this made me think about how Ling was watching me cook because that is how I also learned to cook. She was just there with me.

One day, she surprised me. She offered to stir the soup for me. So, I offered her the spoon, and she took over. I was so excited that I couldn't help shouting, "Yay!"

Ling
I told him to relax.

Lamb
But since I am a very patient person, I saw it as growth. She took the spoon she was stirring the soup, and it showed me how she was growing and learning. It's happened several times since then, and she's even offered to chop the ingredients I needed.

That's how you can see that patience does pay off. Because of my patience for Ling, she started cooking her favorite dishes. That's how I learned to love her mashed potatoes and that sauce she makes that I can eat with anything. She makes rice and mixes it with a bit of butter, and that is something I have never done before.

Patience can lead to baby steps! My biggest ideology is that when anybody learns anything organically, it stays with them forever.

Ling
When people are forced to learn something, it is the first thing they forget after the lesson.

Lamb
That's right. Because Ling has been learning genuinely while watching me cook over the years, there are some things that she can cook very well now. Her magic sauce is proof of that.

My goal is to sit down after twenty years into our marriage, look at each other, and say, "Wow!!! What a beautiful journey we've been on. The world is moving in fast-forward mode–a fast food type mindset. Everything can be ordered with a click of a button and arrive in a few days or even minutes. Everything is so quick and to the point that people are no longer enjoying the process. But I want to remind you to enjoy the process, no matter how long it takes. Be patient with yourself.

Even now, I am still learning patience. We've had to be patient with our brand. There are days when this beautiful wife of mine wakes up tired and does not feel like doing anything. We all have days like that. So, we have learned to be patient with one another even as we continue to manage our social media platforms and my music.

We never force each other into doing anything we're not ready for. Sometimes, we must pull it together for a deadline and say, "Let's just do it." That's a normal part of being an adult and being responsible. When you sign a contract, you must deliver on it.

One of the biggest secrets to our four-year marriage today is that we are truly patient with each other. I'm patient to the point that I will say that if it takes my wonderful wife twenty years to understand certain things, so be it. And she treats me the same.

Ling

It's the act of trying to improve in all things, but especially with patience. For me, it's about just making better progress. I feel much better than I did four years ago. Whether it's when I'm talking with Lamb or responding to things, I know I'm a much better person because of learning patience.

I feel that even my road rage is better!

I used to have no patience on the road. But then I watched a really crazy movie about road rage, and now I'm scared to honk the horn at someone. So, my patience across the board is just doing well now!

Lamb

I'm very proud of Ling, and I make sure to tell her all the time.

Ling

I certainly feel better when I just stop, relax, and tell myself: hold on a second.

Lamb

When you allow your partner to enjoy and take their time to understand patience, they will learn to enjoy having patience because they will see for themselves how much better it feels. Ling has received the totality of wisdom that comes with patience because she sees that it is good for her.

Ling

There are definitely times in our creative journey when we have to focus heavily on the numbers. That's because being a content creator is all about the numbers game. You want to see the numbers grow when you work daily, weekly, and monthly to put out content for all platforms. Your brand depends on it. There were times when we would see our numbers grow and feel that sense of gratitude. But we also had to wait for those really big numbers to appear. We had hopes that our following would become much bigger quickly. This process taught us that it takes focusing on specific analytics to get the bigger numbers on social media. We had to think about regions, categories, and what the brands and managers wanted while balancing our passion for what we were doing and creating. So, this taught us to be patient and not beat ourselves up. Social media is a space where everyone wants to hurry up and hit millions of subscribers and followers. Content creators feel pressured to make quick strides to hit those milestones as fast as possible.

For us, we would sit down together and talk about what was happening with our Ling and Lamb brand. Sometimes, I would vent about how our numbers weren't growing as fast as I thought they should. Or Lamb would express how a video didn't get as many views as we think it could have. These conversations taught us that if you don't employ patience, it can ruin you. If you allow that social media pressure to eat you up and keep you thinking about how to grow your following faster, faster, faster — you'll crumble.

I get that's the type of world we're in right now. I even understand that's how this industry works. Every platform wants you to grow like crazy. If an agent looks at the numbers and sees that you have one hundred thousand followers but no real growth in the last three months, they'll say that you're not interesting because they want to see the increase in numbers.

No matter if you're trying to increase your followers or just succeed in your career, relationships, or personal goals, it is something that you constantly have to reflect on because you don't want it to start interfering with your self-worth and your validation as a person. Just because you don't see the type of progress or growth you want right now doesn't mean it won't happen in the future. Remember to employ patience. Ask yourself:

- *Am I being consistent?*
- *Am I putting in the hours and work?*
- *Am I doing everything that I should be doing?*
- *Am I working hard and working smarter?*
- *Am I trying each day to be a little bit better?*

If you can say yes to those questions, then all you need is to be patient with yourself and your team. You're doing what you can on your end. The rest can only come from what you've put out and patience with the process. This should help you avoid driving yourself crazy.

But if you're only making one post a month, or you're only working on your goals once a month, or you're only networking once a month or not at all, you're not going to grow. It doesn't matter how much patience you have. You'll never grow if you don't put in the work consistently.

Lamb

There have been times when we will put out a video, and I feel the pressure when the new video doesn't get a certain number of views or likes within the first hour. I have to remind myself, and what I would like to share with other content creators, is that life is happening to other people. People are busy with life. They probably haven't picked up their phone yet.

Just exercise patience and know that it's good material. Allow people to be done with their lives as well, and then they will come and like your content. This really helped us as content creators. We both agreed that when we post something,

We were not going to worry about whether it would perform well. We're fine as long as our content is substantive and continues to touch people.

If you've watched us on YouTube, you'll know that we never hustle our viewers to "subscribe now" and all those things. We told ourselves to be patient with our YouTube channel and let it grow naturally. If people watch us and like what they see, they will come back and subscribe. That is why we are not asking our viewers to subscribe now because we have embraced patience.

And look at what happened! Our channel is growing by the thousands every day. We have over one million subscribers on our YouTube channel alone. All because we were patient with ourselves and worried less about the numbers. We are truly grateful for all of our viewers and the comments they leave us. We just want to touch the lives of others, cultivate a community of love, and help everyone smile and live fulfilling lives.

Scan to folllow along on YouTube.

Even though it can sometimes be a lot of work, we are so grateful for what has come of us sharing our story with others. Even though we have been making videos and posts for several years, we still get comments from someone who discovers us and spends the last ten hours watching all of our content. That motivates us to keep sharing our beautiful marriage with others and all of the silliness we get into.

What kind of content do you want to create? What are the next steps of your project? Does it make sense?

If your qualifications can only get you a fifteen-dollar-an-hour job, but you are praying to buy a million-dollar house, the truth of the matter is that no matter how patient you are, that will never happen. The only way that can happen is by looking at other career paths that can lead you to that type of money, like the IT field.

That is patience with wisdom. Many people have been patient but have achieved nothing. While you are patient, constantly reevaluate, reposition, and adjust, even in your consistency.

Don't mix up patience with laziness.

Ling

The formula is the same no matter what you are chasing after. It's patience, consistency, and diligent, clever work, regardless of where you find yourself in the process of achieving your biggest goals. Patience with wisdom is discovering what you need to do next to get a step closer to your dream while remembering that it takes time.

Lamb

Be patient with your partner in general. I fear that a lot of people are not patient with their partners because they allow their cultural belief and societal standards to determine their pace of patience. Personally, I have blocked that out of my way by not listening to what other people say should be happening in my marriage. I blocked that out of our marriage.

By exercising patience with your partner, you'll enjoy your relationship or marriage. Give your partner time to catch up at the beginning of a new relationship. Show them patience when life isn't going as planned and becomes a little tough.

Chapter Seven: Key Takeaways

- There is a difference between knowing to be patient and applying patience.

- Don't misinterpret impatience as rudeness.

- Each marriage has a unique love language. The more I learned about Ling's impatient nature, the more I understood that I could not bring any story about other people's marriages and how they do things into our home.

- Patience, from our perspective, means looking beyond the subject matter.

- When anybody learns anything organically, it stays with them forever.

- Don't mix up patience with laziness.

Share Your Thoughts

In what areas of your life do you feel you need more patience?

- How can you be more patient with your partner?

- How can you be more patient with your career?

- Write it out and start creating a plan to help you achieve your goals and dreams.

Turning Setbacks into Stepping Stones for Success

Chapter Eight

When The Pancake Hits You Back

"I believe in love. I believe in hard times and love winning. I believe marriage is hard. I believe people make mistakes. I believe people can want two things at once. I believe people are selfish and generous at the same time. I believe very few people want to hurt others. I believe that you can be surprised by life. I believe in happy endings."

— Isabel Gillies, American author and actress

Ling

Towards the beginning of our marriage, when we were still living with my parents and I was working hard as an Assistant Property Manager at an apartment complex in Stamford, CT, Lamb and I decided that we were going to try out a new restaurant that supposedly had really good all-day breakfast, specifically pancakes. We make it all the way to the restaurant, park the car, and then.... it happens.
I get out of the driver's side of the car to go inside, and I see that Lamb's not moving. I asked him, "What are you doing?"

He says, "Umm ... is this a good idea?"

There goes my patience right out the window. I sit back in the car and ask him, "What do you mean, is this a good idea? We just drove twenty-five minutes to get breakfast. What do you mean?"

He's sheepish and says, "Well, I don't know. We've never been here. Is it expensive?"

"Lamb, no... we're just getting pancakes. It's not like it's going to be one hundred dollars. And why did you wait until we were PARKED to ask all of these questions?!"

He continues to ask, "Well, how much?"

I didn't even know. At this point, he's freaking me out, and I'm stressed. I pull out my phone to Google it because I'm starting to get scared and the desire to go in has completely vanished. I was able to determine that if we had picked the most decked out and outrageously funky pancakes, it might have been forty bucks at the most, including tip.

Once Lamb realized how much breakfast was going to cost, he admitted, "Yeah, I just don't think it's the best idea. We don't have the money."

All I remember after that is completely crumbling. As I started the car and prepared to drive home, I kept thinking, "What does he mean we don't even have forty f#$%^*g dollars for pancakes? If this is what life is right now and how it will be going forward, I don't want it anymore." I was working forty to forty-five hours a week at a job that I couldn't stand, and I wasn't able to enjoy moments like eating amazing pancakes once in a while?!

The realization later hit me that, really, I was not in the best place to spend forty dollars on pancakes today because in two days, I'll probably have a bill that's due, and I'd be forty dollars short. It was a hard realization where I had to say to myself, "Wow.... I'm in a place in life where I can't afford pancakes." And I truly lost it.

I was mad at myself. I was sad. I was pissed with Lamb at that moment because he was stopping me from getting pancakes — the one thing that, no matter what, will always make me happy (besides pizza). I was upset that we were two broke people and couldn't help each other. I was just mad and upset while feeling that there was no way out.

Money was something that I had struggled with even before I met Lamb. I had watched my parents struggle; I was just tired of all of that sh*t.

That was where I was at.

When we left the parking lot of that restaurant. I remember crying the whole way home.

Lamb kept trying to convince me to pull over till I could calm down, and I probably pressed harder on the gas. I just wanted to race home and disappear. It was so much deeper than just the pancakes. (While I love them, I'm not attached to them.)

I felt a great sense of depression because we were limited in every sense of the word. Missing out on pancakes was the last thing that brought me to a deep realization of our situation. That pancake really slapped me in the face and was a wake-up call. I knew at that moment that something needed to change.

Lamb
───

The situation was truly much more significant than pancakes. I remember that this led to both of us saying we needed to be careful with spending. It was a tough time in our life. We went through a period where we were always eating plantains and eggs because they were cheap.

Ling
───

When we went to the grocery store, we were always looking for the cheapest foods where you only had to add water! We would weigh everything in the produce section to make sure we knew what it was going to cost before we went up to the register. When we bought chicken, we'd get the lightest package, meaning it would have the lowest price. And we would always buy three plantains because they were 3/$1.

Lamb
───

You can imagine how heartbroken we were. For me as a man, I felt extremely helpless. I don't know how many people know what it's like to watch their beloved wife cry in the morning. Then she wipes those tears off, not because there was a solution, but because she has to.

She wipes off those tears, gets in the bathroom to do her makeup, gets in the car to drive off to work like nothing just happened. She gets to the job and does is with grace and elegance, comes back home and literally breaks down again.

That was one of my biggest motivations, and it showed me I was willing to do anything to make money. She was my motivation. Because if I did nothing, we might not be able to pay bills by the end of the month. I can't tell you how many times she would tell me that her bank account has gone negative. Or, that we can't afford to literally spend twenty more dollars as that would put us in a terrible position. We constantly had to wait for Friday, payday. This was a very tough time for us.

I was at home, living with her parents while she was at work. I knew that things were tough, so my goal was to try my best to see what I could do to help reduce the pressure. That was when I started this rule that she never came home to find a bed that was not made.

Ling
With a cute little boy lying on it, waiting for me to come through the bedroom door with a smile on his face. "Bambi!!!" He would always say.

Lamb
I knew that one simple little thing would be therapeutic for her because every time she walked into the room, even though she didn't want to be there, it looked nice. I knew she could feel like this was home.

The other thing I started doing was trying so hard to make sure she didn't come home and worry about food. I would cook with whatever plantain was available in the house or whatever rice, with whatever I could lay my hands on. I would always try my best to mix up something for dinner.

I made these two subtle moves on my own because it was already a difficult time for us. I didn't want to add any more pressure to the situation. Employment at the time was limited because I didn't have working papers or permission and I didn't have an American driver's license nor a car. So, the weight of work fell on Ling's shoulders at the time.

That chapter of our lives humbled us in a special way and even helped us bond more. Whenever she was back home, I would literally start dancing. I would dance down the hallway to greet her at the door or start dancing in the kitchen. Sometimes, I would even sit on the step outside just to watch her car pull into the driveway.

Those were the moments that truly defined our relationships.

Ling
Hard times will either make or break any relationship. Thankfully, they brought us together because we love each other so much. Even now, it's pretty crazy to think about.

Lamb
We were genuinely patient with each other. I didn't have money at the time because I didn't have a job, but not once did my wife ever disrespect me. She NEVER came home from work and started yelling, "I'm paying all the bills! You can't do this or that!" I never lost any form of value as a man. She never made me feel that way.

I am a good man, and Ling knows this. I will never sit at home and capitalize on that situation. I remember having a friend, who was in the same situation at the time. I told him not to abuse his wife's kindness. Everyone has limits.

My greatest fear at the time was not the bills, but I never wanted to get into a position where she would grow tired of me. So even though she told me not to get a job and keep pursuing my dream, I knew that if she had to keep paying for all the bills on her own, in about a year, she was going to go mad. Then, we would truly lose everything.

I loved my dream, but I knew it could wait. I needed to make money. I applied to every home caretaker position to clean homes and care for elderly people.

Ling

He had no car and no driver's license. He thought they should just employ him because of his passion for caring for the elderly, but they said, "Sir, it won't be helping the senior if the senior has to drive you around for his errands." He was putting in the effort to try and make the situation better. It was so cute.

Every week, he would get calls for jobs and couldn't do any of them because we only had one vehicle, and he didn't have a license. I eventually had to tell the companies to take him off their list and stop calling. "Ma'am, remove Lamb from your roster. Thank you. He's trying... Yes, I'm his wife. He's trying to help me. I know it's the sweetest thing, but he has nothing that can help those seniors. Thank you so much."

Lamb

It was such a beautiful chapter of our life. I will forever be grateful for the grace and wisdom in handling that chapter of our life. We never lost focus on our total value. We always respected each other, even in that difficult time. We constantly tried to make sure we helped each other.

Anyone experiencing a difficult time should try to put in the effort. Just keep going.

Saturdays were cleaning days; we would try to do all the cleaning on this day. Eventually, I decided that I, on my own, would do the cleaning, even if I were the only one cleaning the whole house. It was so crazy that her parents would know whenever I cleaned the house because everything was spotless and sparkling like a cleaning person had done it.

I did it because I knew it took much pressure off of Ling. Saturday was the only day she had off work because, by Sunday, she would start hating herself and be immersed in the "Sunday scaries," again, stressing about going back to work on Monday. We only had Saturday. So, my goal, at the time, was to make this a little bit better for her.

If you ever find yourself in the same situation, bury your ego. Bury your so-called standards. Look at things from the factual point of view. Think to yourself, this is my husband, or this is my wife. This is my family. These are the people that would cover my shame. This is us. Just understand that whatever happens to your partner happens to you as well.

A good way to think of it is that we're all going down if I don't play my part. I remember always asking Ling if she was okay because I knew she had a very high pain tolerance. Even when she was smiling, I would still ask her, "Are you okay? Are you sure you're okay?"

Ling

Even when I was a child, I would always say that I was okay. I remember when I was sick but didn't want to tell anyone. Then I remember projectile vomiting all over my mom. It was only at that point that I would confess that I was scared. I never wanted people to know that something was wrong. There is truly something beautiful about hitting rock bottom. It's terrible at the moment, but usually, it turns out, weirdly, to be your best points in life. That's when you're presented with an opportunity to turn everything around.

I know that if I hadn't cried over the pancakes that day, I wouldn't have started looking for a different way to live my life more intentionally. I wouldn't have gone after what I wanted until after that moment. It's hard to think that if I hadn't had that moment or something similar, I could still be in the same place because I might think it's okay. Once you identify that you're in a place where you feel like you can't move forward, it's about reflecting and saying, "Okay, what can I do to turn this around?" Whether you embark on a self-help journey or find ways to better yourself. For me, it was journaling.

I've been a Christian essentially my whole life, so I knew what the Bible taught. But I came across a book that one of my dear friends recommended called "The Secret" by Rhonda Byrne. I thought it was really good and had many Christian roots in it. But they were taught in a different way than I was in a traditional Christian church.

There were a lot of really great nuggets from that book. I also started reading books by Wayne Dyer and Napoleon Hill's "Outwitting The Devil." I began to devour so many self-help, intentional living, and motivational types of books that came into my life at that time. In retrospect, it was probably the worst time of my life. But it really was that pivotal changing point that I needed. After that, I started burying myself in self-help, journaling, meditation, and connecting with God. I was so mad with God for years, and it wasn't until after all that happened that I got into a deeper, better relationship with God.

It was a culmination of those things that brought me to a better place emotionally because physically, I wasn't in a different place. I was still at my parent's house. I was still working the same job. It was my mind that was elevated above my current situation.

Lamb
She started driving around and looking for houses even though we had zero dollars in our savings.

Ling
That's right. We had zero dollars and zero cents in both our savings and checking accounts, but my mind was elevated above that.

Lamb
She booked appointments with realtors, and we would look at these houses as though we could actually afford them! She would point out different things that she liked in each house, and then she would tell me how much all of it cost. I would sometimes have a little panic attack. But it was her way of changing her mindset towards our tough situation.

Ling

That whole year, I started thinking differently, I presented as though I had an 820 credit score, even though, at the time, it was closer to 500 or less. I watched so many things change for us because of the different intentional living practices we put into action.

Lamb

That pancake incident was a hard, yet, necessary reset for us.

Ling

Now we literally go to that restaurant, Chips Family restaurant, at least two or three times a month. Whenever we go in there, Lamb always asks for the best seats. He has to have one of the biggest tables in the whole place. We even bring my parents along sometimes!

But the first time we tried to go there was at the end of 2019. Things had been hard for a while leading up to that point. My journey with self-help, personal development, and all of that started in late February 2020. Right at the beginning of COVID. But for us, as we started living intentionally, things turned around in a few months. It seemed like every month, something new was happening to help move us out of what felt like a bottomless pit.

With COVID happening, I was able to work from home for a little while. Then, I found an office space for the new business idea I had been developing. Ling and Lamb, our brand, happened a few months later. It was in about six months time that everything turned around for us. Lamb even got a job at Lowes, the home improvement store. Lamb took that job as it was closest to the house, which was important as he did not drive, and I was the only driver in the relationship. Thankfully we lived so close, that he was able to walk. It was also the job that had offered him the highest salary.

Lamb ———
I will admit, it took me a while to comprehend Ling getting an office space when we were struggling to afford anything. I know that I wasn't on that same level as she was, but just like I had faith that one day I would marry Ling after just seeing her photo on Facebook, she had faith that with that office space, it would change our lives. She knew it would work out.

I will never forget the reason why I finally agreed to the office space because I was scared. This was the first time she would own something outside her parents' home. Even though I was afraid, I didn't want to kill that dream of hers. I figured, "What was the worst that could happen?" For now, I would support her dream.

Every day after work, she wouldn't come home. She would drive to the office. Our routine changed. She became a different person when she went into the office and would work there till 9 PM. She would do her influencing videos and photos there, her tiara and skincare business, and all her photoshoots.

Ling ———
One of the craziest things is that the woman just leased it to me without any application. It was just another instance where everything aligned because, frankly, it made no sense. I didn't have the money to technically pay, but I was able to make it work. There was no paperwork, and she even let me put less money down for the deposit. She gave me the keys, which was all there was to it. It was crazy.

Lamb ———
That office was the beginning of everything for her because she finally realized that it is possible. She learned to balance the ideology of owning her own business. It's one thing to say you're going to do something. It's another to actually do it.

Chapter Eight: Key Takeaways

- When you and your partner are in a challenging situation, think of the little subtle things you can do to take the pressure off the problem.

- Anyone who is going through a difficult time should try to put in the effort. Just try. It might feel hard at first!

- If you ever find yourself in the same situation, bury your ego. Bury your so-called standards. Look at things from the factual point of view.

- Think to yourself, This is my husband, or This is my wife. This is my family. These are the people that will cover my shame. This is us. Just understand that whatever happens to your partner happens to you as well.

- A good way to think of it is that we're all going down if I don't play my part in this.

Share Your Thoughts

How are you going to turn it all around?

- What certification or degree do you need to get into the career that you want?

- Consider where in the world you would want to live to be close to the type of job you want or the type of people you would like to meet.

Intentional Living ———————————

Chapter Nine

You Had The Power All Along

"You've always had the power, my dear, you just had to learn it for yourself."

— Glinda, The Wizard of Oz, 1939 Film

Lamb ──────────────────────────────────
This is an important chapter. You'll want to read this chapter without distraction and with a notebook in hand.

Ling ──────────────────────────────────
The "Wall of Abundance" was something that I started doing right away when I initially read The Secret in February 2020. I created it on the Wall of Our Bedroom while living at my parents' house. It was something that helped me to visualize everything that I wanted to see. So, anything that I wanted to manifest in my career, for my happiness, what I wanted to see in my family, and what I wanted to see transpire in real life, I put it on the wall. It all needed to be tangible to make the Wall.

Scan to watch the video.

When I understood the power of visualization, I grabbed a bunch of magazines. It was like my scrapbooking era when I grabbed home, clothing, modeling, and celebrity magazines. I just started cutting them up and putting them on my wall. I put on the wall all I wanted to accomplish in my lifetime, and I wanted to manifest it as a daily reminder.

I had always grown up with church lessons about dream books and things like that. But there was something for me about doing a wall where I could see it visually every day. When I was getting ready for work every morning or leaving the house to do anything, I could look at it, stare at it, and keep that visualization in my mind.

I held onto those images so deeply that I genuinely believed I would achieve everything on that wall in my lifetime. And I still believe that because not everything is ticked off yet! This helped me in many ways *because of that current space I was in.*

The bedroom in my parents' house wasn't much bigger than 100 square feet, maybe even smaller. It was the space I shared with my husband, where the bed really took up most of the space. We opened the door and pretty much fell onto the bed. So, it wasn't a very big space. Yet, I could visualize all of these big goals I had for myself. Knowing that I was telling myself living with my parents wasn't permanent made it easier to deal with my current reality.

Creating the Wall of Abundance was beyond just putting images of what I wanted on a wall and daydreaming about it all. It was figuring out how I was going to take what I was looking at and plan out the steps I would take to get to it. That's where the intentional part comes in.

I may have subconsciously done this in parts of my life years prior, but I've never done it in such a concentrated manner to make it my new way of living. This wasn't something that happened immediately. It was a practice.

I don't think it's easy to look at a wall with a four-million-dollar house on it, be broke on Monday, yet on Tuesday believing that I'm going to have that very house one day soon. I knew that if I was ever going to get to that point in my life, not only would I have to live intentionally, but I would need to implement a lot of patience, patience, and patience. My Wall of Abundance fueled my intentions. They became the things that I was affirming for myself. I did this with the knowledge that it's going to take work on my part.

I also know how to be patient with myself in getting there. Along with the four million dollar home, I also included rejection emails from brands I wanted to collab with at that time, my bad credit score that I wanted to improve, places I wanted to go and explore, businesses I wanted to start, a postcard from an old job that states "lifesaver," because I feel God put us all on this earth to help one another, and that's what I always want my life to reflect helping others. These additions were crucial to my board and really helped me grow.

Lamb

I'm a realistic guy. I firmly believe that if this bill in my hand is five dollars, it is five dollars. I can hold it. I can feel it. I see it. The Christian religious background I grew up with taught me that we create hope. I knew how to pray but was not taught the true principle of intentional living.

There have been times when I have waited, sometimes for several years, hoping that my prayers would be answered. I have known what it feels like to be brokenhearted and disappointed when what I was hoping for never happens. This is why I have become a very realistic person.

When Ling started the wall of abundance, it was the first reminder I'd had in a long time to take part in prayer and hope. I had a massive wall between me and opening up to the idea of a Wall of Abundance because I would not go down that rabbit hole again. I've fallen victim to it before. Therefore, I did not care about it.

I used to look at her, literally, look at her and think, When she's done being crazy, she will let me know. I wasn't going to say anything. I was not going to tell her no. I just thought the whole idea was crazy. So, I let her go crazy by cutting up things and putting them on the wall.

If you go back and look at that wall, you'll see that she has put 99.9% of everything on it. The only things I put on there are the blank check she gave me to fill out and a dollar note.

Even though I thought Ling was crazy, she is still the person I love dearly. She is still my wife. What I love about how she did this Wall of Abundance is that she didn't force it on me. She approached this like I would come along when I was ready.

But I remember she said this one thing that made me question my position on the whole Wall of Abundance idea. I don't know what we were discussing, but it turned into an argument. And I'll never forget when she said, "If you don't believe, then don't stand in my way. You can hold onto your realistic way of thinking, but don't get in my way."

I thought about what she had said and agreed not to hold her back from what she was trying to do with her affirmations and intentional living. This was my first initial moment of understanding her point of view and what she was trying to accomplish. I gradually started looking at her and began to appreciate what she was doing.

I started to tell myself, "If this is truly going to happen, then I'm going to have to get a job." This added more pressure on me to find a job that would support our goals. I had to learn to balance fate with reality. I see this four-million-dollar house even though I don't have four dollars in my account!

I approached finding a better job by looking at careers that paid well. I started looking into becoming a data scientist because I thought, "How do we make this kind of money?" I was willing to develop the skills to take us closer to the dream on the wall of abundance.

Ling
He took one class, and he was done!!! But I did appreciate the effort he was putting towards this idea. Even though he knew nothing about data science, he was still willing to take the courses just so we could get to where we needed to.

Lamb
This is where the intentional living aspect started to creep in. We had determined that our goals were reasonable, but we also knew that you don't just walk around and find a bag of money on the floor. I had to think, "How do we realistically position ourselves to receive that blessing?"

Ling then started doing so well with our savings because she was making more money then. We started gradually experiencing the shift, even though we lived in a single bedroom. It was all about becoming very intentional.

This shift happened within us as well. When certain things could not happen because of our finances, we simply let it go. It didn't bother us like it used to because we were not living intentionally with goals in mind.

I remember when somebody gave us a late wedding gift. It was something like a thousand dollars. We didn't even need to talk to each other. It went straight into the savings. So you see, it became almost second nature and subconsciously changed our lifestyle. We were clear on our goal, and then we became intentional in making sure we put together every little thing we had.

Ling

Getting there, however, was a bit of a process. Lamb had to unlearn what he had been through and what his experience was with having hope. The issue had been not pairing it with intentional living, and that's what I started to teach him.

One way I taught him was by giving him a blank check. The idea is to write an amount on that check that you believe will push your faith. It is an amount you really want to manifest, even if you don't know how you will reach it.

So I wrote a check out with my number, $1,000,000.00!!!! and then I gave Lamb his own check. I told him, "I know you're having a little bit of a struggle with this, but I want you to take this check, and when you're ready, fill it out with an amount that you believe is the number for you." The point is to pick a number that will one day wow you when you receive it.

It was not an immediate thing for Lamb. I had to ask him a week later if he still had the check and if he had filled it out. Once he finally came up with a number and filled out the check, I asked him if he really believed it. I explained that filling out the check doesn't matter if you don't believe it. That's the whole idea behind visualization and manifestation.

The whole idea about trying intentional living is honestly believing that what you want to achieve is your actual reality and existence. I believe it is how God intended life to be. When Lamb told me that he believed, I knew he meant it. We prayed about it, and then put his check on the wall of abundance. To me, that was his initial breakthrough. Once he did that, it was like it had made it easier for him to start putting his faith out there in a larger capacity.

Another thing I did was give each member of my family an actual mustard seed. I put each one in a little jar for them to have so they could carry it with them and have a daily reminder of just how little faith they need to move mountains.

Lamb
I still have mine, and I carry it everywhere I go.

Ling
Mine broke, so I must make another one, LOL! I ordered the seeds and the jars from Amazon and assembled them. If you didn't know, the mustard seed is one of the tiniest seeds in the world.

Lamb
That was the first time I had ever seen a mustard seed, even though I knew the story well and had heard it many times. Seeing that little seed in the tiny jar hit me differently because I could see it and think, "This is all God requires from us."

This was not Ling trying to force me into this lifestyle journey with her. She said, "Can you just give your faith as little as this mustard seed."

That was a game-changer. From the day she gave me the mustard seed, everything changed and it became even more apparent what was needed from me in the sense of spirituality. This was the final step of alignment that we needed on that journey.

That's why I still have it, and it will never break. I carry it everywhere I go, and I travel with it. We were in a meeting in Atlanta, and I brought it there. I was sharing the story of why I carry it with other people. It's been years now that I've been having that with me. With that mustard seed, I finally changed my mind about everything.

Ling

That is why it's essential to set tangible goals for yourself with intentional living. Journaling. The abundance wall. Putting things on your mirror. A mustard seed in a jar that you can actually hold in your hand. When it's just a thought, there is nothing that you can grasp. When you make something or write it down, it becomes real. You can touch it and see it. This helped Lamb on his journey as a realistic thinker.

Lamb

The foundation of every action is sitting on an intention. If I pick up a bottle of water and start drinking, the drinking part is the action. But what was my intention? I intended to quench my thirst. Intentional living starts from looking at yourself, looking at your partner if you have one, and realizing that you truly are heading somewhere.

You must be very, very, very intentional about every aspect of your relationship and your life. Think about the intention behind every action you take. For example, if a couple feels they are too focused on money or greedy, they can then focus on acts of service.

Looking back on some of the things I've done, whether it was trying to take classes or build up my skill set, it was all with the intention of one day having a career that would lead my beautiful wife and me toward accomplishing our goals and dreams. That is how I support our belief system. With intention behind every action.

Starting a lifestyle based on intentional living is looking at the overall significance of your existence.

Ling

A good way to create intentional living is by assessing the different aspects of your life. You can intentionally change how you exercise and the way you like to move your body. I started implementing Pilates into my morning routine, and it's been really, really amazing for my all-over body strength. My body feels better now, and my knees feel better when I go on walks. My legs feel stronger, and I can walk longer as I also spend this time focusing on my spirituality with prayer. This is all from intentionally changing this one aspect of my morning routine. If you think about it, there are many ways to apply intentional living:

- *Health*
- *Emotions*
- *Exercise*
- *Education*
- *Finances*
- *Spiritual*
- *Nutrition*
- *Routines*

Lamb

I know many people who were in the same situation as us who would just eat any junk food or super cheap food. But even in that situation, we were very intentional with what we ate because we didn't want to end up having to see a doctor. So, we became very intentional about being healthy.

That is how intentional living includes every aspect of you. If you're deliberate about your savings and career but leave out your health and spirituality, you'll never move in the direction you want to go. It's all tied in.

The revolution you need — the transformation you want to change your life — is embracing the whole meaning of intentional living.

Ling

One of my favorite all-time quotes is from Glinda, the Good Witch from The Wizard of Oz 1939 film. "You've always had the power, my dear; you just had to learn it for yourself." I've been obsessed with that movie ever since I was little, and I'll never forget, at the very end, after all that Dorthy's been through, feeling hopeless, to be told she had the power all along. Just click your heels, and you can do what you want. For Dorthy, it was to get home. That was all she wanted.

I thought of that as I started going through this lifestyle change. I was making little changes and setting my eyes on different goals. Some of them were small, and some of them were bigger. And each time I reached a new goal, I was like, Wow! I was able to do that. I have had the power to make the life I want to live. It feels like unlocking a new level in a video game!

I know it sounds crazy, but things started happening almost immediately when I started living like this. I don't know, maybe it was God's way of being that ray of sunshine we desperately needed. I was so done with our situation, and after what I experienced, I truly hope that everyone who starts living intentionally will hopefully experience the same immediate results. That's how the law of attraction works - positive thoughts bring positive results into a person's life.

It happened quickly, which is why it encouraged me to keep going. As I continue to live this lifestyle, I know there are things on my Wall of Abundance that I haven't achieved yet. So, I have to either keep exercising that patience or go back to my drawing board and say, "Okay, am I doing enough to get there?"

If I've assessed that I'm doing enough, then it's just about patience. I believe that in many cases, when you haven't reached something after a year or more (most of the time), there is something that you can tweak. To be honest with myself, there is one goal I want to reach, but I know I haven't done enough tweaking to get there seriously. If it happens, it'll be because I put it out there and I'll recognize it as a profound blessing. But to achieve it, I know there is another level I need to unlock. But I need to do it. I don't feel discouraged because I know what needs to happen next. For anybody who feels discouraged in their pursuit of their goals and dreams, you have two options. Either keep trying because you want a different result, or you can give up and stay in the same place that you are in. The thought of staying in the same place is often enough fuel to keep trying.

I truly believe that something will happen if you stay consistent with the intentional living lifestyle.

Lamb

People who struggle with intentional living might have the wrong mindset. It's not a lottery you can win that can magically happen by purchasing a cheap ticket. You still have to do the work every day.

You must understand that if you truly want to become very intentional, you have to embrace all the shapes and forms of humility. A lot of people can look at intentional living and think it's fabulous, but their ego and pride get in the way. Sometimes, this can become an internal war where the person doesn't even know that they are the problem, and instead, they try to blame God or the universe, or whatever else but themselves.

Based on my own experience, when Ling started on the whole Wall of Abundance and intentional living, I had to humble myself. I had to look at it from the angle of not approaching this from my past experiences. Humble yourself and let it just flow.

If you ever find yourself in a difficult situation, ask yourself:
- Am I letting my ego get in the way?
- Am I letting my belief system get in the way?
- Am I letting my past experiences get in the way?
- Do I not truly believe?
- Have I at least given faith the size of a mustard seed?

Make sure you clear all of that, and then you might be shocked at how you solved your problem all by yourself.

Ling

You must be willing to open up to something different. Most people aren't living intentionally naturally. Even more are not aware of the benefits of intentional living. It is a practice and something that doesn't happen overnight.

My experience is based on the fact that I worked fast to immerse myself in this lifestyle change. I was so done with my current situation that I wanted to reverse it quickly. I feel like it's not always that fast for some people. Different things hit different people at different times; life is always happening. I've learned that consistency is needed to keep me going and to lead me to more productivity.

Lamb

The truth of intentional living lies in answering the question: How badly do you really want this? Everyone says they want to be successful, but how many hours of good production do people complete each day, one hour, or perhaps nothing was accomplished in their day? If you want to know how much you could have done on a given day, just wake up one day and look for a highway around you. Notice the cars that are flying by as early as 5 AM. Many of us don't even wake up until around 7 AM. You must understand that life starts at 5 AM, and people are already out there getting on with their day, working to be productive.

Ling

As with any practice, it is necessary to keep it up daily. I usually leave the house at some point every day for a walk to be out in nature and get plenty of fresh air. That's my meditation time. That's the time I like to pray.

I haven't been journaling as much as when I started, but I still like to write down different things or place sticky notes with affirmations around the office. I used to journal every morning at work and did so for an entire year and a half. Now, I have this jar that I call a "wish jar." I write down things that I am thankful for and also things that I want, and then I roll them up and put them in the jar.

I still do that because getting what's in your head out on paper is important. It'll help you visualize it differently.

Another thing I do daily is to constantly stay in a positive space so that I can receive positive things. This is not to say that there are days when I'm not happy or that I'm a little bummed and not feeling so great. I am not super 100% positive every day.

But when I want to be open to receiving good, I have to be in a good space and have a positive mindset. This is my daily reminder as I continue to practice intentional living. Eventually, it just becomes a part of me. Now, I don't have to tell myself, Let's meditate. Let's go pray. It's just who I am now.

On days when I'm not the most intentional, I absolutely feel a little bit off. I don't get upset; instead, I accept that something can get done at a different time of the day or on another day altogether. But for the most part, this lifestyle is ingrained.

Lamb
———
For me, it has just carried on. When you genuinely live intentionally, it becomes a part of your lifestyle. I no longer sit down trying to say I need to be intentional. Instead, it is like I've built a system. Now, I'm functioning in this system. My belief is still the same, but now I see how it's easy to keep going when I am intentional about what I do daily.

It is possible to live intentionally and start to see those blessings in your life but then get distracted. You can lose your control of that continuity. Always try to remind yourself where you were and what got you started in the first place. Remind yourself why you never want to go back.

I never want to be back in a place where my wife will say she wants $40 pancakes, and I have to tell her no, we can't afford this.

Ling
———
No, we never want to be back in a place where the pancake has to hit us in the face again!

Lamb
———
That is the biggest motivation ever to keep the practice of intentional living going.

Ling

Since creating the wall of abundance, we've both become self-employed. That was one of many things on our wall. I always wanted to be my own boss. We created a brand and have seen it grow and expand in a way that isn't typical. It's very unusual for the brand that we've built in this space to develop the way that it has. Most other brands that talk to us often tell us that our growth is unprecedented without a celebrity boost or a video that goes viral with millions of views overnight.

We truly grew the Ling and Lamb brand, which speaks to our intentional living practices. Putting the idea on our wall of abundance, seeing it first, and then working towards it has been a very rewarding experience. Other things along the way include the health goals that have been reached, tests passed, and financial goals that we wanted to see happen - have happened. We've been able to take some great things off the wall, for which we are thankful.

We accept that, thank God, and move on to the next goal. It's a beautiful thing to see it manifest from thought in your mind into a tangible thing you've written down or a picture you've cut out and stuck in a place you can see every day, then to see it manifest in that physical way - it's the most incredible feeling ever.

This is how possible it is for people who started literally from the bottom to change their lives solely by implementing intentional living.

Lamb

Intentional living is beautiful. It's like a magnetic force. Things will start coming to you. Sometimes we look at each other like, "How did we get this job?" Ninety-nine percent of the jobs always come to us, and we can't really explain the mechanical forces that place the work in front of us. We often wonder what the email sender saw that made them want to contact us. We don't know what they heard. We don't know what made them feel that Ling and Lamb is a good fit for their campaign.

We don't know how that happens, but we firmly believe it happens because we've positioned ourselves in a particular space. We're very intentional and clear. Our hearts are pure toward each other and everyone. It's attractive because it brings goodness.

I know people who believe in intentional living, but they want to know how it's going to happen. None of us have the power to tell how it will happen. Instead, we just have to have an open mind. That gift might arrive in a box that you least expected it to.

Chapter Nine: Key Takeaways

The idea behind intentional living is that you honestly believe what you want to achieve can and will be your reality and existence. It's essential with intentional living to create tangible ideas for yourself.

- Journaling
- The abundance wall
- Putting things on your mirror
- A mustard seed in a jar you can hold in your hand.

- When it's just a thought, there is nothing that you can grasp When you make something or write it down, it becomes real. You can touch it and see it.

- The foundation of every action is sitting on an intention.

- Intentional living starts from looking at yourself, looking at your partner, and realizing that you are in this with someone and both of you are heading somewhere.

- The truth of intentional living lies in knowing,

- "How bad do you want this?"

Share Your Thoughts

How can you start living intentionally?

Itemize it all. Ask yourself realistic questions.

- What am I doing now?

- What value am I bringing to the world?

- What are the problems that I am currently facing?

- What are my strengths? Take the time to recognize these as well.

- What do I want for myself and what changes do I want to see in my life?

- What steps do I want to take to get there?

The Power of Words

Chapter Ten

What You Say Is What You Get

"Words are seeds that do more than blow around. They land in our hearts and not the ground. Be careful what you plant and careful what you say. You might have to eat what you planted one day."

— *Unknown*

Lamb

I'm a big, big fan of the fact that there is power in your tongue, and because of that, I've always been very, very careful of the words that I use. Even before I met my wife.

I feel like I manifested Ling even before I came across her picture because I've been saying it for years. For example, I used to pray for my marriage. I used to bless my future wife even before I knew who she was. I used to say, "Whoever my future wife is, I bless you. I pray that you are healthy. I pray that life is treating you well wherever you are in the world." I was sewing that seed of a happy marriage for years. Even when I was in a relationship that I wasn't sure about, but knew it wouldn't end in marriage.

Human beings are designed to always project their beliefs and thoughts upon their fellow human beings. It is left to you to either accept or reject it. I believe that it takes a plus and a minus to align for a battery to function. When society, family, and friends project their negativity or belief upon you, if you don't accept it, it will not manifest.

There is a quote that I use even when I go to the prisons and speak to these men and women who are behind bars. I say to them, "What you allow is what is allowed, and what is allowed is what becomes."

I remember when we were first married, people said that we were now in the honeymoon stage. Our response was, "Nope." This is not just a stage in our life when we would love each other like we first did. We both agreed that we will love each other like this forever.

I believe this is one of the things that makes our relationship so unique. We don't base our marriage on what other people think, and we love each other as we do. Our response to other people's opinions of our marriage is, "Don't project your marital beliefs on us."

This power of the tongue also relates to how people talk to themselves. People can look at themselves and literally tell themselves, I cannot be great or I'm a failure. There are many ways in which you can talk yourself down. And if you keep telling yourself those things, eventually, they will manifest.

What you say, applied with your strategic and intentional movement, will give you either your expected results or at least close to your expected results. For example, if you look at the NBA, there are so many NBA players – but there are very few great ones. The great ones have something in common. They said they wanted to be the greatest, and then they did the work. They practiced while other people were sleeping. They put in a different level of energy to become the greatest.
The day you begin to understand how powerful your tongue is is the day you know the meaning of "be quick to listen and slow to speak." Your words are your powers.

Ling ───
Words are powerful in how you speak to others and yourself. My positive mindset came in 2020 when I changed to live more intentionally and be a more positive person.

I was much more inclined to be positive because I realized it's human nature to default to negativity easily; it's just the easier thing to do. We are surrounded by it with the news or social media, so it's easier to be negative than positive.

Positivity for me started the year I began my journey with intentional living. Before then, there were still plenty of positive moments in my life, and I didn't consider myself a super negative person. But when I became more aware during the journey, I realized, Oh, wow! That's not good to say that about myself! Maybe that's why things haven't changed. Or, It's not good that I say that about my body. Whatever it might be: body, skin, or hair.

If I keep telling myself that I'm having a horrible hair day for an entire week, no wonder! That's what I've been telling myself every day for a whole week. Those are the words I think or say, and that becomes my attitude and my reality.

Unkind self-talk was something that I used to do a lot. I still have to catch myself sometimes. But because I worked on my positive mindset, I feel now it is more natural to be positive. I feel so much better about myself because I'm in a more positive space. That was the big switch because I saw negativity immediately before the positive side of things. That was a huge contrast for me, and I didn't start until I became more aware of it. Sometimes, it's wild now to listen to how people describe what is going on in their lives. "Oh, my car just always breaks down." Why is that? Because that's how that person always describes their life. If that's what you say, then that's what will happen.

Or the person who often says, "I'm sick again, so we have to cancel. You know me. I'm always sick." Why is that person always sick? Because that's how they describe themselves. That is what they are always saying. It's crazy the power of words.

The things we say about ourselves, sometimes daily, we don't even realize how powerful those words are. What you say about yourself and your life is literally what will be and continue to happen.

Just like the saying: you are what you eat. Same thing with words. Whatever you say will eventually happen.

When you realize the words you are using and determine if they are more negative than positive, that is how you can automatically switch them. I realized that after being naturally pessimistic in my self-talk, the only other way was to try positivity to change my circumstances.

Lamb
―――――――――――――――――――――――――――

It's almost like being sick or going to the doctor because something is not right, and it's the moment the doctor names it, then it takes root in your mind. Because the doctor has said it out loud, the name alone can hit you harder than the disease itself. People have died from a name alone because the word of the disease completely defeats you.

Some people fight psychologically with words. The great boxer Muhammad Ali would talk to his opponent before a match, and he literally knocked them out before entering the ring. It's how he looked at his opponent and the few simple words he says to really mess with the guy mentally. This just goes to show you how powerful words can be.

Ling
―――――――――――――――――――――――――――

I've always heard the saying, "This is a man's world." I took it as there is no real place for a woman in high places, authority, or essential positions. And while I knew that is what society sometimes says, I never experienced that personally because I never allowed myself to think I was any less capable than a man.

I can do anything a guy can, and potentially better, as long as it doesn't require physical strength because I know the science involved. Can a guy pick up something heavier than me? Maybe, maybe not... if I've been training.

But the point is that reality is only what you accept. So, I never accepted what society said about this being a man's world. In every job I've ever had, I've always worked in a position that men could hold. It showed that the position wasn't only for men. And there have been times that I've worked hard to get higher positions where men were in positions below me. So that's how I proved what society says is not always the case because I didn't accept it.

Lamb

Society has this thing they do a lot — starting with age. Society feels your career is dead once you are above a certain age. They feel like you cannot become as successful as you would be if you were younger.

I've seen this happen in the entertainment industry with my music. Since I've been singing and creating music for a long time but haven't had a particular breakthrough, society might think that my time is now gone. But I look at myself and say, "No, my time has not gone!"

I will admit that there was a time when I almost allowed society to tell me that I should just forget about my music. I'm so happy that I picked myself up again and told myself my talent has no expiry date.

But as long as I keep opening my mouth and recording and singing, I don't care if two, three, or five people want to hear my music. There will always be somebody out there willing to listen to my songs. And someday, somebody might be one hundred million people.

Even as we are writing this book, I am a huge surprise to many people because society says that I'm done. My music career is over. Yet, I've stopped listening to what people say. I'm still recording music, producing albums, and creating music videos.

For the first time ever, one of my songs hit 1.5 million streams. Just imagine if I had allowed society to stop me with their words. I wouldn't have known that on the other side of the wall, a song was waiting for me to record that would one day be a huge success.

Always remember that society will project their fears. Even people who couldn't achieve their dreams will try to project that failure onto you. But you are not them. Your destiny is different. You are all on a different journey. No one is ever on the same journey.

You are on a personal journey, no one else's. Just keep your head up and just keep going. Never allow people's projections to affect you.

Instead, let it be the coals in your fire to keep blazing.

Ling

Lamb is always complimenting and flattering me. Literally, there isn't a day that goes by that he doesn't say something at least once, but usually from the time we wake up, throughout the day, and until the end of the day, "My fine girl! My beautiful girl!" When he's talking to someone, it's, "My beautiful wife!"

Even if he doesn't know I'm home and I've just walked through the door and gone through the house, I'll hear part of his conversation, and he'll still refer to me as his beautiful wife when he doesn't even know I am there to hear him say it.

I believe any wife would want to hear those things from her husband and vice versa. Guys love hearing that, too. It's nice to hear a positive affirmation. I really enjoy it when I put in the effort to do my hair or make-up a certain way, and Lamb notices. He compliments me. That is so special to me, and I also think it is unique.

I know not all couples do that. We receive comments or emails from our viewers who will write, "I love the way that Lamb speaks to Ling. My husband doesn't do that for me." Or, "I love the way that Ling speaks to Lamb. I wish my wife would tell me I'm handsome and give me facial treatments."

One guy sent us a DM that almost made me cry. He wrote, "I wish I could get my wife to love me the way that Ling loves Lamb." It made me sad, but it was also so sweet that viewers pick up on the fact that we treat each other well. While I know we're not the only couple on the planet who are this way, I do think it's very unique and rare. I genuinely believe this is a great way to be in a serious relationship. It's not "being whipped" or "being a simpleton" or "being too in love." This is what a healthy relationship looks like, acts like, and breathes like. How we talk to and complement each other is so special, and I really appreciate it.

We've only been married for four years. Some people have been married for thirty-plus years and never talked to their spouse like Lamb and I talk to each other. I've been in relationships where the 'spark' seems to stop after three months.

To have somebody who sees you day in and day out for four years, married, knows you're there 'forever,' totally becomes comfortable — and never stops complimenting you like it's the first date. That's something I'm very grateful for, and it shows how powerful words are and how they can make you feel.

Lamb
I agree with Ling, especially how I feel a lot of men will stop complimenting or saying affirming words early into the relationship. I will never forget the day Ling told me, "I love you, and I want to spend the rest of my life with you." The feeling that came over me was that feeling of something so desired, something I wanted so much, the beautiful gift I was hoping for, and now it is mine. That feeling is something that I will never forget.

Chapter Ten: Key Takeaways

- Human beings are designed to always project their beliefs and thoughts upon their fellow human beings. It is left to you to either accept or reject it.

- What you allow is what is allowed, and what is allowed is what becomes.

- What you say, applied with your strategic and intentional movement, will give you either your expected results or at least close to your expected results.

- The day you begin to understand how powerful your tongue is is the day you understand the meaning of *be quick to listen and slow to speak.* Your word is your power.

- The things we say about ourselves, sometimes daily, we don't even realize how powerful those words are. What you say about yourself and your life is literally what will be and continue to happen, like the saying, "you are what you eat." So, mind your words; whatever you say will eventually be as you say.

Share Your Thoughts

How are your words?

Take this time to write down some of your limited beliefs about yourself that might be holding you back. Then, what are the opposite statements you can start to believe in that are much more positive?

> *Example: "My body is so chubby." Instead, you can say, "My body is strong and helps me get through the day."*
>
> *"I am so tired all the time." Instead, you can say, "I've been working really hard lately. Let me take some time for me to recharge."*

Also, think about the words you say to others. What words do you use when speaking to your spouse or partner? When was the last time you complimented them and gave them words of affirmation to lift them?

When you notice the words you are using, determine if they are more negative than positive.

_____

_____

_____

_____

_____

_____

_____

_____

_____

Happiness in a Social Media World

Chapter Eleven

Not All That Glitters Is Gold

"If you're looking for the next big thing, and you're looking where everyone else is, you're looking in the wrong place."

— Mark Cuban, owner of the Dallas Mavericks

Lamb

To be completely honest, we don't even remember to record 80% of the moments that crack us up. We don't even remember to get the camera to snap a photo. We just enjoy ourselves. In fact, I would go as far to say that Ling laughs all day long. Only in the morning, she probably wouldn't laugh! But I'm changing my game plan to get her to laugh in the morning, even when she doesn't want to talk.

All that glitters is really gold for Ling and me. We are sincerely true to ourselves; even when we have misunderstandings, they are minor. When we sit down and talk about it, we always resolve it. As much as possible, we try to ensure that what we see on social media is our true selves.

Ling

With social media, I believe, people post only the good to give a fake representation of their reality. Or you might have experienced what it was like to follow someone on social media only to find out their life really isn't like what they post. There are even times when I wonder what viewers might think of our good relationship and debate whether or not it is as they see it because of so many fake posts on the Gram.

That's our thing, though. It is exactly what you see- good and not-so-good moments. It's not the edited pictures or the scripted videos. It is simply our spontaneous life that we try to share with the world, and the message is that true love is possible, and this is what it looks like.

Lamb

Social media is a market square where everyone wants to bring their best products and display them for sale. A lot of times, what you have is well-edited and well-scrutinized. Before they post the picture, they've probably taken a thousand to find the best angle. Most people just look at these things and assume that is exactly how life is.

Nobody sees the back end. Nobody sees how many swipes

you went through in your gallery before you said, "I'll post this one." Nobody sees how often the cameraman snapped a picture of you or how many editing apps were used to get the perfect image.

Now, you may wonder how to find your true self in that space. How do you make sure you don't end up getting depressed? It is too easy to wake up daily and compare your life to others you see on social media, but you can also be insecure. How do you make sure you are not a social media slave?

It's simple. As a family, couple, and best friends, we genuinely enjoy each other's company. We truly crack each other up. Everything you watch or read about us is who we are. I would say that even some of the best moments we don't even remember to record. We're comfortable and happy with ourselves, which is one way to survive watching others on social media and not letting other "perfect" lives bother us.

So many times, we say to one another, "Oh, wow! We should have captured that moment." That tells you that out of twenty-four hours in a given day, we only share a few seconds, 58 to be exact, with our viewers—only one minute, maybe two minutes on special days, with the world. But the remaining 23 hours are spent being beautiful together, enjoying ourselves, eating food, and playing - this makes us happy and fulfilled.

Just know that before you believe someone is your mentor on social media – find and know yourself first. Find what makes you happy first. Find what completes you first. Let that become an element of motivation. Then, see if the person you chose to be a mentor is a strong fit.

That is why we pray. Ling prays every day for others. Even though she is very independent, she is also emotional and prays for our followers often. When she sees messages or comments like, "I wish my wife loved me like this," or "I wish my husband would love me like this," it breaks her heart. She prays for people because what we share on the Ling and

Lamb platform is genuine, and we want everyone to experience the same love we have for one another.

If we were not honest with our viewers, I am sure that Ling would not be able to feel the way she does. But she can feel their pain and wishes they could feel and experience what she enjoys because that is her reality.

While living with Ling's parents, we started posting to social media in our one-bedroom. A lot of people will not even post or share those moments because it is different from their standard of what they want the world to see. Looking back, we never let our situation deprive us of enjoying that stage of our lives.

Ling

There is no manual on how to survive and navigate the social media space with sanity. It's a new and ever-evolving space that can be amazing, yet also ridiculous at times and very overwhelming. There's a lot of comparison complex.

The minute you get on, you're flooded with imagery of people living lavish lifestyles, driving luxury cars, owning designer bags and fancy accessories, or having huge houses. All of that is pushed out to you, forcing you to see the glitter and the gold, which is easy to be attracted to. Sometimes, it can put you in a bad space because you may not have the same things. That is why it's essential to be sure of who you are so that you feel validated. So when everybody else is glittering, and their gold is shining - whether or not it's real - you are content with yourself and all you have!

A lot of people are putting on a facade on social media. But whether it's real or whether it's not, you can't allow it to seduce you and make you feel bad. The rates of depression right now, especially social media-based depression, are crazy high. More people today are seeking help from therapists because their anxiety is horribly high. It is too common to know someone who suffers from panic attacks compared to ever before. That is because people feel like they're crumbling under this pressure to be the best, and no one posts their progress. No one posts their bad days. No one posts their challenges while trying to make it through their journey. They only show you what they want you to see.

You have to remember to be strong in your mind and know that you've got this. You know truly what glitters isn't always gold. Yes, that person might have a huge house, a beautiful car, or other expensive things, yet they might be really sad. They don't have somebody to go home to every day. They might not have a family.

You might see someone posing with their car, but the reality could be that it's getting taken away next week. You won't see that update. So it's always important to feel strong and safe in your own reality. That's a real key point to stay strong and know that you don't need to let the pressure of everybody else's glitter get you down. Instead, let that motivate you to get where you want to be.

Or, just turn it off. If the social media space is too much for you, step away. Sometimes, people have to get off of it for a long time. It really depends on what you are using it for. Being very secure in yourself is the starting point for managing it safely.

Lamb and I get comments, emails, and a lot of direct messages like, "Oh my goodness, you guys are such a breath of fresh air. I can see genuine love and laughter. There's something different about you guys." That's what we wanted to bring to people. Even when you catch us on a live stream, we are just being our authentic selves.

It's funny when we're doing a livestream, and we tell the audience that we were upset with each other just a few seconds ago, we're trying to be honest and let them know every day is not perfect in our relationship.

and that's how real we are with our audience. We had a podcast for a short time, and are looking forward to picking it back up.

When we think of social media, we want it to be a happy space where people know they can come to and get actual content, substantive content, and be a part of a community that won't make them feel that glitter is gold complex.

Lamb

We are not a platform that sells get-rich-quick schemes. If you follow us on our platform, you'll see our pictures and videos showing that it took time and hard work to get to where we are.

The beauty is that many of our followers have followed us since we were in Ling's parent's house. They've seen our growth and progress. We used to do our YouTube from where we used to cook and all of that. Those followers have watched us move out of the house to our first apartment. They've stayed with us, seen where we are today, and will join us for where we will go next.

You'll never feel that we just came out of nowhere because we have a track record to show you - showing that success takes time. So, if you see us in a big mansion tomorrow, or whatever it is that God blesses us with, you won't feel depressed. I think you'll be inspired because we are transparent with the process and the effort that goes into the process.

When we got our first big deal with Crocs, we shared our excitement online. We said, "Oh my God, we just made the first amazing check." Our followers and viewers see these things. We want them to have that level of information about us.

If you are sincere with yourself and feel that there is a mentor or people online who inspire you, observe them and notice their process. Embrace their process. But you can't say they inspire you if you're unwilling to embrace their ideas and feedback and join in on the hard work needed to succeed.

We have people that we look up to. We don't just look at where they are. We look at their history. We can honestly say that we are on the right track because ten years ago, they didn't have this, or five years ago, they were not like that. That's how we measure our process and progress to those we look up to.

When you find yourself scrolling social media, don't just focus on the image or video just posted; instead, understand the process, the journey, that person, that creator, that celebrity, or that public figure used to get them to that post.

One of my biggest inspirations when I got to America is now one of our good friends. His name is Giannis, and he's an NBA player. Giannis Antetokounmpo inspired me like crazy because of his story. In fact, it was Ling's dad who told me his story. He said, "There is this guy in the NBA, and he's Nigerian. I think you should pay attention to his story."

When I discovered him, I didn't focus on him making hundreds of millions of dollars playing basketball. No, I focused on how he did that. I focused on his journey. Like how he got to New York. How did he survive? How did he get there? Then I compared that to where I was, and that's how I knew I was on the right track.

Today, he's a good friend of ours. He's a big fan of Ling and Lamb. That is a good example of how we saw the glitter and glamor and let it inspire us. We saw him become a champion, which was a huge inspiration. He still inspires me every day.

Ling

It might feel necessary for some people to implement parameters on screen time. It's a feature that Apple rolled out, and maybe Android has it too. Or perhaps it is something that you don't even need an app to do. You can make a mental note that you're only on Instagram for maybe an hour a day or on social media for just a few hours daily. That way, you will not be constantly overloaded.

People don't realize that we can overload ourselves on social media. If you're already struggling with that glitter is gold complex, trying to figure out if it's real or not — consuming it more will not help you, especially if you haven't gotten it under control yet.

It's always good to put a certain number of barriers around screen time. With us, navigating social media is our occupation. Sometimes, we agree to put our phones down to avoid overload. Don't live on social media; don't let it run you.

You control it. It's an app that is there for your use. You can do your business, connect with family and friends, and receive news. It should not consume or take over your life.

Lamb

When using social media, follow other people who motivate you. If you have someone on your social media page that depresses you – unfollow them! Instead, follow people who are honest with their stories and journey. Those who are transparent.

The power to follow and unfollow is in your finger. If you ever feel that a particular person on social media makes you feel uncomfortable or a certain way, activate your finger and click unfollow.

Too often, people come out of nowhere to tell people they've made a million dollars, and every post they create is them holding money. They get so many followers because they have money. Not because they have shown the journey they went on to make that money or show that it's even real.

If it weren't for Ling, nobody would even see our apartment. We received a lot of pressure from our followers to do a "house tour," but I don't like those sorts of videos. We don't like being flashy. If it weren't for that demand from our followers who have seen our journey, we probably wouldn't have done a tour video. It's not something we want to put in people's faces.

Ling

I love how our platform has grown to inspire others. If anything new and exciting happens in our lives, we share it on our platform. We don't rely on any other press. We only share what inspires us and show how we've grown. Along the way, our viewers and followers have grown, too.

Lamb

Ask yourself. Why are you on social media? We know we are there because part of it is work, and we enjoy it. We are aware that God has blessed us with our platform. On my personal page, I promote my music and prison reform efforts; Ling uses her page to promote her modeling, and then we have our Ling and Lamb platform. We are clear on why we use it. You now have to ask yourself why you use social media.

There are certain people that I will never follow on social media. If I mistakenly find them on my feed, I block them because I don't want that energy. It's that simple. You have that same power to control your own social media experience. You can control how it makes you feel.

People need to pay more attention to the value of what is available around them. They don't see it. They always think that there is something else out there. No! The good is right there in front of you.

It's like holding a screwdriver. If you don't understand the power of a screwdriver, it's a useless tool. But to the person who genuinely knows what a screwdriver does, they'll know how it works when they see one.

Everything around you is extremely valuable. So, find peace and contentment at every stage of your life. What you see on social media should not depress you or make you feel you are missing out. Instead, be grateful for the things around you that you can't find on a screen.

I've said it before, and I'll continue to say it. This beautiful woman right here never loved me any less when we lived in a bedroom of less than 100 sq ft. She has never changed, and I appreciate that.
This is what I mean by finding peace in every stage of your life.

Don't underestimate the tools that you currently have. For example, when we lived in that room at Ling's parent's house, I wanted to record a song. I couldn't afford to go to the studio. So, I recorded it on my phone. I would go to the voice recorder, open it, and tape my vocals because that phone was all I had. Guess what? Nobody knew the difference - it worked!

Other people would have been depressed or cried because they could not record in a studio. Yet, I recorded my songs and even shot videos with my phone. Ling helped me record while I performed when I couldn't pay a director.

I'll never forget when we walked through Walmart, the lights flickered. The light was broken, but it gave off a vibe that Ling picked up on. She saw the shot as I stood in front of that light while she recorded.

We used what we had. That video came out amazing and beautiful.

Ling ──
Attitude of gratitude unlocks all the good things.

Lamb

We drink, eat, sleep, and wake up in gratitude. That's us every day. When you understand that you came into this world with nothing and one day will leave it with nothing, it makes sense to view life differently. It will help you appreciate everything.

Using that perspective, you must begin to enjoy every stage you find yourself in. Life is beautiful. Life is sooooo beautiful. I had to unlearn a lot of things to see life truly. So, don't complicate it.

Ling

Focusing on being grateful almost immediately fixes my attitude, especially on social media. Maybe I'll see something I don't have yet regarding my goals, but I'm thankful it's coming to me. And in the meantime, I'm happy with what I have.

Remembering what you have, even the smallest things, will always bring you to a good place — and a place to receive more. When you wake up grateful, it helps you to see the things you might not have had before. It puts you into a great headspace and allows you to receive more into your life that you can be grateful for.

Lamb

Because our society often celebrates big news, big events, and big happenings, it shifts society so that when small wins occur, they're not recognized. You find out that many people are walking around and not even realizing how many wins they have each day. All because it came in a tiny package. It didn't come with a big red ribbon for them to cut, with people celebrating everywhere.

I hope people will pay the same attention to the small wins as the big ones. Every win is a win.

Chapter Eleven: Key Takeaways

- Find yourself first. Know what makes you happy first. Find what completes you, and that becomes an element of motivation. Then, look for your mentor on social media who shares your goals.

- You have to remember to be strong in your mind and know that you've got this. You know, honestly, what glitters isn't always gold.

- If the social media space is too much for you, step away. Sometimes, you have to leave it for an extended period. It depends on what you are using it for. Being very secure in yourself is the starting point for managing it safely.

- When you find yourself on social media, don't just focus on the present image or video posted. Respect and understand the process, the journey that person, that creator, celebrity, or public figure took part in to get to that post.

- It's always good to put a specific barrier around screen time. With us, navigating social media is our occupation. We still have times when we agree we must put our phones down because we don't want to overload.

- Don't live on social media; don't let it run you.

Share Your Thoughts

So now ask yourself: Why do I use social media?

Conclusion

"It is only when we take chances, when our lives improve. The initial and the most difficult risk that we need to take is to become honest."

— Walter Anderson, American painter and writer

Lamb

Before we begin this chapter, you must know that I'm looking for food to eat. Yes, writing a book and looking for food at the same time is possible.

A lot of times, you fall in love with the shining, beautiful elements of your partner. I remember the first time I saw Ling. It was in a beautiful photograph, and I fell in love. In fact, I somersaulted in love. I wasn't hearing anything anybody else was telling me. The moment for me was so strong and attractive. Everything said about her went in one ear and out the other because I was drawn to her.

As much as I was drawn to Ling's image, I was still looking for a connection. I remember the night I was going to fly back to Nigeria, I asked Ling to pray for me. She had not even agreed to date me yet. I just asked her for a prayer because I was trying to see if there was a connection outside the attraction. It took me a good five minutes to convince her to agree to pray for me. She laid her hand on my chest and started praying.

I felt a deep level of peace that I could not explain. That was a more profound connection that solidified everything you are seeing today. I've held onto that memory and that feeling, and now it has become a part of me. I'm very protective of that feeling. I'll never forget what that special gift represents. Even though Ling is a strong, independent, and beautiful woman, I'm still protective. It's not work. It's not complicated. It is what it is because I never lose sight of those values.

I'm very protective of her because I know what she represents. I value our relationship and love, even if we sometimes joke about how protective I can be.

Ling

Like when I want to go for a hike, he says, "You cannot go on a hike by yourself anymore." I tell him to leave me alone!

Lamb ———————————————————————————

That is just my protective instinct. I just want to make sure that my baby is okay.

This is not just another girl that I am hanging around with. Ling is someone very, very, very, very valuable to me. I don't play around.

I even don't let certain people talk to her on the phone. When people call me to ask, "Uh, can I say hello to your wife?" I'm like, "No. No, you cannot say hello to my wife."

Complimenting her and continually choosing caring words to describe the feeling and everything, keeping it very intentional, has become a part of our lifestyle. We are here together, and I am trying to reinforce the value of our marriage.

Marriage is not meant to be good for the first and second years and then become a struggle for the next ten years before returning to those first loving feelings. No! No! No!

I still wake up, and if I don't see her, it's like that feeling from the first night I slept beside her. Every morning, I look for her. I did that this morning.

Ling ————————————————————————————
And I was downstairs doing Pilates.

Lamb ———————————————————————————
Even after four years, I still look for her every morning. When you truly understand what it means to have someone who loves you, looks out for you, protects you, fights for you, and sacrifices with you, you don't take that for granted. Nothing should allow you to take that for granted. Not your job. Not your colleagues. Not a phone. Nothing.

I know it's not easy. Life happens sometimes. Maybe you're famous. Perhaps you have a busy job. Maybe you have a position at work where people rely on you. Perhaps you have to deal with other people throwing themselves at you.

That is why the foundation of a relationship has to be solid. Don't lie to yourself. Be completely truthful with yourself. Ask yourself, "Am I really into this person? Do I really love this person? Can I stand the test of time with this person?"

The key to having a successful marriage is ensuring that you have a peaceful home. How can you make sure that you continually have peace in your home? That's all there is to it. For me, it is an immense privilege and something I don't take for granted to be with someone who has decided that they want to spend the rest of their life with me. Nothing should ever make you take a love like that for granted.

Negativity is very, very loud. The reality is that toxic relationships are being praised. Many people fall victim because what you hear is what you dance to. But if you hear positive things, you dance to positive things.

But it is important to know that before you start chasing after a couple of goals or looking for answers on social media, you should truly understand that there is a deeper level to everything you see on the outside. You must honestly know yourself first, genuinely and sincerely. That is where you'll find your answers. That is where you'll prepare to chase your goals. First, you must look inside yourself.

From a masculine point of view, I want to drop some words of wisdom. Pride and masculine sentiment will deprive men of truly experiencing love on a very deep level. Some men might see what Ling and I have and believe they can't experience it because they fear acting silly.

When I see Ling's dad interact with his wife - it's beautiful - he acts like a kid! They've been married for 37 years, and although he is a strong man, he's like a baby around his wife.

Not all men can enjoy their homes to their full potential because they are masked with the idea that they must act a certain way to be the 'man of the house.' This is a good example of a generational belief that has been passed on but is a bit outdated.

All men need to do is flip the switch in their minds. Look at your wife not as a commodity, but just look at your wife as the best partner you could ever have. Ling is my better half. She is my baby. She is not a woman just waiting around, here to cook for me, have my kids, or clean my house only.

The other day, we did a video where I said, "Anything you cook, I will eat it." Later, when I was reading the comments online, we realized that a lot of people had picked up on that one thing I had said amongst everything else that was going on in that video. There were a couple of comments like: Oh my God! That is so sweet!

That's my way of letting her know I appreciate what she does for me. Even though it might not be my thing, and it's not my favorite it's the thought that counts. I will tell you that there are a million and one men who don't think like that. Once that mashed potato is not the way they like it, it's garbage to them.

To my fellow men, I say: just try. Try to achieve a beautiful home for yourself.

The other morning, I randomly caught Ling sliding in her socks on the floor as if she were ice skating. As she did that towards the kitchen, I immediately thought, My baby is *happy*. It might not have been a big deal, but in that second, she was at peace in our home—that is the goal for every marriage.

Ling

For the women reading this book, take care of yourself and be good and even better to others. Women tend to do many things for friends, mothers, relatives, spouses, coworkers, and bosses. Sometimes, we do so many different things that we, as women, can lose our identity and, ultimately what makes us happy.

I've heard many women say they have lost themselves in their husbands' dreams, careers, or children's goals. It's one thing or another that always leads to them losing themselves. That natural instinct to be caring and nurturing leads to an "I have to do everything" complex. It's very easy to do.

My most extensive advice to women is to focus on themselves to be a better person for themselves and those in their lives and find what makes them happy. Because when you do that, it's like you are unlocking the next level of your life. As you discover your own happiness, imagine a key sliding into your own lock and truly unlocking your full potential and beautiful foolishness.

We'd like to take this time to thank our readers and viewers from over the years. We hope we've given you some helpful hints on applying and finding happiness in your everyday lives. One of the things we are considering is creating a podcast where we break down each chapter of the book and discuss it more in-depth. Let us know if you think that would be something you'd like to hear from us.

Lamb

While this book contains the story of our marriage and happiness, it is now time for you to take what you learned and apply it to your own life! Consider this moment: How do you make the helpful hints in this book applicable to your reality? If your relationship is not at a great place, begin to look at yourself and do a reality check truly. How can you build your own beautiful foolishness, or at least be on your way to building your own beautiful foolishness?

Ling ──

A time of introspection is needed to find a way to apply these takeaways in your life. This book is a great tool that you can return to time and time again even if it's just the key takeaways at the end of each chapter, or the special places you've marked, or the pages where you've folded the corner of. When you are going through a tough time, you can return to this book to focus on one particular chapter at a time.

Acknowledgments

Lamb

My gratitude sincerely starts from my family. I send my deepest gratitude to my parents, and my grandparents on both sides of the family. Growing up among such a diverse ethnic group, my family shaped me into who I am today. How I pronounce things, how I say things, my beliefs, and my traditions. Everything. It is why I am so open to loving someone not from my continent because of my diverse background.

My gratitude goes to everyone who, in one way or another, has impacted me. To those people I stayed with when I left home as a teenager. I lived with a lot of families and friends, and I borrowed their shoes or jackets. Some lent me their books for school. All of them shaped me.

I want to thank the community of Lagos, Nigeria. That positivity and fighting spirit is something I will never forget.

I also want to thank everybody who ever told me "no" on my journey. This propelled me and pushed me to be better in life. All of those doors that were slammed in my face kept me going. I knew that someday I would get there. So, I thank them.

I want to say a very, very big thank you to my wife. It is crazy to think about meeting somebody who is a total stranger and falling in love with them. You listen to your emotions. You begin to build a life with them. You begin to learn to live with them. You begin to learn to talk to them. Everything.

Ling has made our home very peaceful. I do my part, but at the end of the day, it is like the saying, "The woman in your life will either make or break you." I couldn't have asked for a better partner to do life with. So, I want to say a huge thank you to her.

I would also like to thank Ling's parents for always encouraging me.

I was a young man from a different country, trying to find my way around. They gave us a roof over our heads while we were beginning our marriage. No amount of money can pay them back.

And to our Ling and Lamb fam. I love every single one of you! And we are grateful that we see all of you from all walks of life come together and just love our love language. Love has no color. It knows no boundaries or classification. Once you feel it and know it, you go for it. We are so grateful for our fam from TikTok, to YouTube, Instagram, Facebook, and all future platforms that have yet to be created.

I'll round out by saying, "Thank you, Ling." Our love is free. There is freedom in this relationship. We are able to give each other the very best. This marriage is a journey we've never gone through before, but we are building it together.

That is it. I want to go and eat.

Ling

My acknowledgement will probably be a fraction of Lamb's because he's the one who is always talking. I want to acknowledge and thank my parents for everything. For being amazing parents who helped shape me into the woman that I am today. Also, to my brother and grandmother. We've always been very close, and I'm thankful for the impact that has made on my life.

I'm very thankful for all of the experiences that I've gone through in life. It was crazy, but I'm grateful for all the moments that brought me to where I am today: the good, the bad, and the ugly. I'm thankful for all of it.

I'm so grateful to the Famington for finding the place in the community that Lamb and I created. A place of love, happiness, and acceptance. I am so grateful to the fam for finding a home here and accepting us because we are all about acceptance.

What might be one of the last, but it's probably more like the first - I want to thank God for every single thing. Without God, there would be none of this.

Lamb ———————————————————————————————
Oh God! Did I thank God?

Ling ———————————————————————————————
Did you? I don't think you did!!!

Lamb ———————————————————————————————
Woooowwwwwwwllll! I must put it first! Forgive me, Lord! I was thanking all your children.

Ling ———————————————————————————————
Let's see if you get forgiveness after I finish. So yes, I would like to thank God for everything you've done in my life, and I'm just glad I recognize you and remembered.

Lamb ———————————————————————————————
Please, Lord. I will remember you and share all my food with you.

Ling ———————————————————————————————
Lord, I'm so grateful you've always been there for me and seen me through everything. You always protect me. Thank you for your love so that I can love and give love to others. I'm very grateful to God. Of course, that wasn't the last person. The person I would like to acknowledge especially, and who I am grateful for is my Bambi. I love my baby Bambi, and I'm so thankful to do life with him. I'm so appreciative

to unlock the next level of life with him. He's just so amazing. There are no solid words I can use to describe how thankful I am for him.

Lamb

Let's make mashed potatoes now.

About the Authors

Ling and Lamb have stolen the hearts of their rapidly growing fanbase with their genuine love for one another and enthusiasm for everything they do. Given Ling is from the U.S. and Lamb is from Nigeria, their different experiences in life and cultural clashes provide a much-needed daily pick-me-up. This is why they've amassed more than 130M likes on TikTok, YouTube is generating more than 750K views per day with over 1.57M subscribers, and across all platforms, they have over two billion views since they started creating content at the end of 2020. Their viral videos focus on lifestyle moments, foodie content, pranks, and relationship + love advice.

Their growing fan base consistently requests a Ling and Lamb Food Tour & Reality Show, which has ignited the next chapter of the Ling and Lamb brand. They are taking this show on the road for a tour where Ling and Lamb will try all sorts of new, fun, and interesting foods to share their genuine reactions with their fan base while still tying in the lifestyle and authentic experiences that Ling and Lamb's fans are so accustomed to seeing.

Ling and Lamb have made on-camera appearances on the Kelly Clarkson Show, NewsNation, and News 12 CT + NY. They have been covered by Buzzfeed, People, PopSugar, India Today, and CT Insider.

www.ingramcontent.com/pod-product-compliance
Lightning Source LLC
Chambersburg PA
CBHW021148160426
43194CB00007B/744